THE PHYSICS
OF ANGELS

Also by Matthew Fox

Letters to Pope Francis: Rebuilding a Church with Justice and Compassion

Occupy Spirituality: A Radical Vision for a New Generation (with Adam Bucko)

Hildegard of Bingen, a Saint for Our Times: Unleashing Her Power in the 21st Century

The Pope's War: Why Ratzinger's Secret Crusade Has Imperiled the Church and What Can Be Saved

Christian Mystics: 365 Readings and Meditations

The Hidden Spirituality of Men: Ten Metaphors to Awaken the Sacred Masculine

The A.W.E. Project: Reinventing Education, Reinventing the Human

A New Reformation: Creation Spirituality & the Transformation of Christianity

Creativity: Where the Divine and the Human Meet

Prayer: A Radical Response to Life (formerly *On Becoming a Musical, Mystical Bear*)

One River, Many Wells: Wisdom Springing From Global Faiths

Sins of the Spirit, Blessings of the Flesh: Lessons for Transforming Evil in Soul and Society

Passion for Creation, The Earth-Honoring Spirituality of Meister Eckhart (formerly *Breakthrough*)

Wrestling With the Prophets: Essays on Creation Spirituality and Everyday Life

The Reinvention of Work: A New Vision of Livelihood For Our Time

Sheer Joy: Conversations with Thomas Aquinas on Creation Spirituality

Creation Spirituality: Liberating Gifts for the Peoples of the Earth

The Coming of the Cosmic Christ: The Healing of Mother Earth and The Birth of a Global Renaissance

Illuminations of Hildegard of Bingen

Original Blessing: A Primer in Creation Spirituality

Meditations with Meister Eckhart

A Spirituality Named Compassion

Confessions: The Making of a Post-Denominational Priest

Hildegard of Bingen's Book of Divine Works, Songs & Letters

Whee! We, Wee All the Way Home: A Guide to Sensual, Prophetic Spirituality

Religion USA: Religion and Culture by way of TIME Magazine

Manifesto for a Global Civilization (with Brian Swimme)

Passion for Creation: Meister Eckhart's Creation Spirituality (formerly *Breakthrough: Meister Eckhart's Creation Spirituality in New Translation*)

In the Beginning there was Joy (children's book, illustrated)

Western Spirituality: Historical Roots, Ecumenical Routes, editor

Also by Rupert Sheldrake

A New Science of Life: The Hypothesis of Formative Causation

The Presence of the Past: Morphic Resonance and the Habits of Nature

The Rebirth of Nature: The Greening of Science and God

Seven Experiments That Could Change the World

Dogs That Know When Their Owners Are Coming Home

The Sense of Being Stared At

Science Set Free / The Science Delusion

Also by Matthew Fox and Rupert Sheldrake

Natural Grace

Exploring the Realm
Where Science and Spirit Meet

THE PHYSICS
OF ANGELS

Matthew Fox · Rupert Sheldrake

Monkfish Book Publishing
Rhinebeck, New York

We gratefully acknowledge permission from The Shrine of Wisdom, Fintry, Near Godalming, Surrey, England, to quote from their English translation of the writings of Dionysius the Areopagite, and from Cambridge University Press to quote from the English translation of the *Summa Theologiae* of St. Thomas Aquinas, originally published by Blackfriars, in conjunction with Eyre and Spottiswoode, London. We thank Tom Barnes for translating many of Hildegard of Bingen's texts.

Originally published in trade paperback by HarperCollins in 1996. Monkfish Book Publishing trade paperback edition, 2014. First ebook edition, Monkfish Book Publishing, 2014.

Cover image: "White Light" © 1999 by Alex Grey, acrylic on wood.
Book and cover design: Danielle Ferrara

Library of Congress Cataloging-in-Publication data

Fox, Matthew.
        The physics of angels : exploring the realm where science and Spirit meet / Matthew Fox and Rupert Sheldrake.
        ISBN 0-06-062864-2 (pbk.)
        1. Angels. 2. Angels—History of doctrines. 3. Physics—Religious aspects—Christianity. 4. Photon—Miscellanea. 5. Pseudo-Dionysius, the Areopagite—Contributions in doctrine of angels. 6. Hildegard, Saint, 1098-1179—Contributions in doctrine of angels. 7. Thomas, Aquinas, Saint, 1225?-1274—Contributions in doctrine of angels. I. Title.
BT966.2.F68   1996
235'.3—dc20   96-12696

Monkfish Book Publishing ISBNs:
Paperback: 978-1-939681-28-7
Ebook: 978-1-939681-29-4

Printed in the United States of America

Monkfish Book Publishing
22 East Market Street, Suite 304
Rhinebeck, New York 12572
www.monkfishpublishing.com

To the Angels
In the hope that they return to guide us

Angel

1. A ministering spirit or divine messenger; one of an order of spiritual beings superior to man in power and intelligence, who are the attendants and messengers of the Deity; hence *b.* one of the fallen spirits, who rebelled against God; *c.* a guardian or attendant spirit; *d. figurative*, a person who resembles an angel in attributes or actions.
2. Any messenger of God, as a prophet or preacher; a pastor or minister of a church; *poetical*, a messenger; *figurative*, in *angel of death*.
3. *transferred*, A conventional figure with wings.

(*The Shorter Oxford English Dictionary*, Oxford University Press, 1975)

Photon

A corpuscle or unit particle of light.

(*The Shorter Oxford English Dictionary*, Oxford University Press, 1975)

A quantum of electromagnetic radiation that has zero rest mass and energy equal to the product of the frequency of the radiation and the Planck constant. In some contexts it is convenient to regard the photon as an elementary particle.

(*The Penguin Dictionary of Physics*, Penguin Books, Harmondsworth, 1975)

Table of Contents

★ ★ ★

Preface

★ ★ ★

It may seem unlikely that a scientist and a theologian would discuss angels in the twenty-first century. Both disciplines at the end of the modern era appear equally embarrassed by this subject.

Nevertheless, although angels have been ignored by the scientific and theological establishments, recent surveys have shown that many people still believe in them. In the United States, for example, over two-thirds believe in their existence, and one-third state that they have personally felt an angelic presence in their lives. Half believe in the existence of devils.[1] Angels persist.

We are entering a new phase of both science and theology, and the subject of angels becomes surprisingly relevant again. Both the new cosmology and the old angelology raise significant questions about the existence and role of consciousness at levels beyond the human. When the two of us held our first discussions on this subject, we were fascinated by the parallels between Thomas Aquinas speaking of angels in the Middle Ages and Albert Einstein speaking of photons in this century. Hence the title of this book, *The Physics of Angels*.

---

1. "Angels Among Us," *Time*, December 27, 1993, 56-65.

The grassroots revival of interest in angels is timely. Much of the present interest centers on experiences of help and assistance at times of need. It is intensely personal in nature, and individualistic in spirit.

Recently we have both had the privilege to sit down with Lorna Byrne, the Irish peasant woman and grandmother, still illiterate, who has now published three books on angels with whom she has been in contact since she was a little child. She was instructed not to tell of her encounters until given the word, and that word came after her husband died. Her books rapidly became bestsellers world wide, having appeared in at least twenty-six languages at the time we write this preface. It was clear to us both while speaking with Lorna that she is as authentic as they come, a true "sod of the earth" of green Ireland, direct and matter of fact, joyful and hard working and generous.

But she insists that the angels have some important messages for us today, messages of their disappointment in the paltry advances we have made as a species and, surprisingly enough, messages about the role America can and needs to play in the world's spiritual awakening—a role based on the fact that in America so many religious traditions have gathered and interfaith practice is most developed. In her most recent book *A Message of Hope from the Angels*, Lorna emphasizes how "we all have a part to play in the spiritual evolution of humanity."

Lorna prefers being interviewed in "interfaith events" rather than giving public lectures. One such event occurred in New York City at St. Bartholomew's Episcopal church when black Baptists, Jews, Buddhists, Hindus, Christians, and Muslims gathered for her public interview. Also present at the event in New York, she tells us, were angels who "packed the chapel" and she reports that "there was great joy and celebration among them at this wonderful gathering of different faiths." The angels were as pleased as she was because people had come not to convert each other but with open hearts in order "to listen, to pray, and to celebrate, and not to justify their own religion or to claim that it was superior."

Lorna's descriptions of angels as "balls of fire" parallels some of Hildegard of Bingen's visions that we relay in this book while treating her writings on angels. Also, Hidlegard tells us that angels praise human work, and Lorna too makes many references to angels' appreciation of the work that humans do—and might do if we were to wake up more fully—to contribute to the advancement of our evolution, one that takes us beyond reptilian brain "I win/you lose" dynamic to an authentic practice of our deep interdependence with one another and with all of creation.

I, Matthew, am very aware of Aquinas' teachings that angels "carry thoughts from prophet to prophet" and that angels "announce the divine silence" and that angels "can't help but love" and that angels learn exclusively from intuition, so as we develop and honor our intuition more we may well be running into angels along the way. And that they assist us in many ways including the unfolding of the process of evolution. When I met Lorna I shared some of these teachings from Aquinas and she very much seconded them based on her experience, and she has underscored them also in her books on angels. Great things can happen with the help of the angels.

How about you? Do you sense the angels among us? Do you encounter the "speck of light" (Eckhart called it the "spark of the soul") that is within us all. If so, what is its message? What are we needing to learn? Hopefully this new version of this book will continue to ground angelology in a substantive discussion from both religious and scientific perspectives of what angels are busy trying to accomplish with us humans in these trying and significant times.

THE TRADITIONAL UNDERSTANDING
OF ANGELS IN THE WEST

The traditional Western understanding of angels is much deeper and richer than the more individualistic modern angel literature would suggest, and far more concerned with community and our common development and our relationships with one another, God, and the universe. These values fit with a more holistic or organic understanding of nature and of society.

Furthermore, it is important to acknowledge common experiences that emerge in all world cultures and religions when we are living in an ever-shrinking global village. All cultures, including our own, acknowledge the existence of spirits at levels beyond the human. We call them angels, but they go under different names in other traditions (Native Americans call them "spirits"). Angels constitute one of the most fundamental themes in human spiritual and religious experience. It is difficult to imagine deep ecumenism or interfaith advancing among the world's cultures and religions without acknowledging angels in our midst and angels in our own traditions.

Other experiences that all human beings face together include the ecological crisis, for which we require all the wisdom we can muster. Angels may be able to assist us in this work and may well prove to be indispensable allies, truly *guardian* angels, instructing us in *safeguarding* our inheritance of a once healthy but today endangered planet.

For all these reasons it is important to return to our own spiritual tradition to examine what it tells us about angels, and to connect that wisdom to today's evolutionary cosmology. This is necessary in order to set the stage for deeper explorations in the future—a future we believe will be characterized by a more eager effort to examine consciousness on this planet and beyond.

To assist us in this task of exploring our own spiritual tradition, we have chosen to concentrate on three giants of the Western tradition whose treatment of angels is particularly broad, deep, and influential. They are Dionysius the Areopagite, a Syrian monk whose classic work *The Celestial Hierarchies* was written in the sixth century; Hildegard of Bingen, a German abbess of the twelfth century; and St. Thomas Aquinas, a philosopher-theologian of the thirteenth century.

Dionysius the Areopagite made an amazing synthesis of the currents of the Neoplatonic philosophies of the Middle East in the light of his own Christian theology and experience. Hildegard of Bingen, though she called on the tradition of angelology handed down through the monastic tradition of the Western church, nevertheless worked especially out of her visionary experiences with the angelic realms. Thomas Aquinas created a synthesis of the study of angels, including the views of the Muslim philosopher Averroës, the writings of Dionysius the Areopagite, the science and philosophy of Aristotle, and the biblical tradition. He also raised profound, speculative questions that are provocative even today, and are especially interesting in light of the cosmology now emerging from today's science. It is likely that these three thinkers devoted more of their intellectual labor to angelology than any other three major thinkers of the West.

We begin with an introductory dialogue in which we explore the history of the understanding of angels in the West and the way in which they were central to the tradition of the early church and medieval theology. We explore how the mechanistic revolution in science in the seventeenth century left no place for angels in a mechanical cosmos and led to a decline of interest in this subject in science and theology. We also discuss the recent grassroots revival of interest in angels (surely Lorna Byrne's work is part of this movement) and the importance today of an ecumenical and interfaith or cross-cultural understanding of the spiritual realms.

We then turn to our three main authors. We have selected their most important and relevant passages about angels, and each of these passages is followed by a discussion in which we try to work out their meaning today from both a theological and a scientific perspective.

In these discussions we are less concerned with the theology and science of yesterday than with the potential theology and science of tomorrow. We have both found this method of dialogue illuminating. It has taken each of us beyond any understanding we would be able to arrive at individually with our own limited perspectives. We hope that what for us was a creative process will help others in their exploration and thinking.

We conclude by considering how the exploration of angels in a living cosmos could enliven and enrich both religion and science as we enter a new millennium. We end with a series of questions.

An appendix of biblical references is provided for those wanting to study the scriptural examples in greater depth and detail.

Introduction

★ ★ ★

The Return of the Angels and the New Cosmology

Matthew: Why are the angels returning today? In recent years they have been the subject of many magazine articles and TV shows, and there is a flood of books, including several bestsellers, about angels. Is this a fad? Are angels just the latest consumer object for hungry souls? Is this a flight to another world, an escape to an ethereal realm of light, a distraction keeping us from addressing pressing social and political issues?

Or might it be that the return of the angels can inspire our moral imagination? Can they give us the courage to deal more effectively and imaginatively with these issues as we move into the third millennium?

In the 1990s I took a survey, asking people if they have ever experienced angels. Between 60 and 80 percent of the people at my lectures say that they have. Perhaps such people are not typical, but surveys of random samples of the American population show that a third have felt the presence of an angel at some time in their lives. This suggests that angels do not always have to be believed in. When you experience something, you do not have to believe in it any longer; it's not a matter of belief but a matter of experience. Mysticism is about trusting our experience. And today, perhaps we are being asked to trust our experience of angels.

In the machine cosmology of the last few centuries, there was no room for angels. There was no room for mystics. As we move beyond this machine cosmology, no doubt the mystics are going to come back, and the angels are returning because a living cosmology is returning. St. Thomas Aquinas, the thirteenth-century theologian, said, "The universe would not be complete without angels. ... The entire corporeal world is governed by God through the angels."[2] The ancient, traditional teaching is that when you live in the universe, and not just in a manmade machine, there is room for angels.

What is an angel? And what do they do?

First, angels are powerful. Do not be deceived by the bare-bottomed cherubs with which the Baroque era has filled our imaginations. When an angel appears in the Scriptures, the first words are, "Don't be afraid." Now would those be their first words if they came as bare-bottomed cherubs? "Pin my diaper on," would be more likely. But angels are awesome. The poet Rilke says that every angel is terrifying. What are they powerful at?

Angels are essentially understanding beings. They think deeply. They are experts at understanding—at standing under. The primal thoughts that uphold all our other thoughts, angels know through intuition, according to Aquinas and other teachers on angels. Angels don't have to go to school to learn the essence of things. They don't need discursive reasoning and experimentation to learn. They get it all intuitively, immediately.

They are experts at intuition, and they can assist our intuition. This is one reason that angels and artists befriend one another so profoundly. When we look at the wonderful, amazing images of angels that artists have given us, we are dealing not with just a rich subject of

---

2. *Summa Theologiae* 1, q. 50, a. 1; q. 63, a. 7.

painting but with a relationship going on between angels and artists. Intuition is the highway in which angels roam.

Angels are also special friends to the prophets, and we need prophets today. We need prophets in every profession, in every role of citizenship, in every generation. We need young prophets and old prophets. "What do prophets do?" asks Rabbi Heschel. "Prophets interfere." If we are going to shift the course of humanity today, we need prophets, and, according to Aquinas, angels are very much involved in prophecy.

In addition, angels have very strong wills, and Aquinas says, "Their will is by nature loving." Angels are not abstract intellectuals; they are loving, understanding beings. Loving invades their understanding. Their knowledge is a heart knowledge. It is wisdom, not just knowledge.

And so we see that in their expert domains of understanding, knowing, loving, compassion, and prophecy, angels clearly have a lot to teach us about spirituality. And their tasks are not trivial. They have serious cosmic duties to perform, relating to the wisdom and the knowledge that they carry. One of these tasks is to praise. Wherever there is praise going on, angels seem to show up. Indeed, I think their absence parallels what I would call a praise crisis in Western civilization. As we learn to praise again, the angels will return.

Both Hildegard of Bingen and Thomas Aquinas teach that the devil does not praise, and that's what makes the devil different from the angels—a refusal to praise. How much of our culture in the last few centuries has indeed been a refusal to praise? What is praise, except the noise that joy makes, the noise that awe makes? And if we are bereft of praise, it is because we have been bereft of awe and joy in the machine, cagelike world we have been living in. The new cosmology awakens us again to awe and wonder, and therefore elicits praise.

To study angels is to shed light on ourselves, especially those aspects of ourselves that have been put down in our secularized civilization, our secularized educational systems, and even our secularized worship system. By secularization I mean anything that sucks the awe out of things.

The angels are agents and co-workers with us human beings. Sometimes they guard and defend us; sometimes they inspire us and announce big news to us—they get us to move. Sometimes they heal us, and sometimes they usher us into different realms, from which we are to take back mysteries to this particular realm. Aquinas says, "We do the works that are of God, along with the holy angels."[3] But even more than that, Aquinas warns us that angels always announce the divine silence, the silence that precedes our own inspiration, our own words, the silence that meditation and contemplation bring.

Angels make human beings happy. It is very rare to meet someone who has met an angel who doesn't wear a smile on his or her face. To encounter an angel is to return joyful. As Aquinas says, happiness consists in apprehending something better than ourselves. Awe and wonder and the kind of power that angels represent are of such an ilk. They call us to be greater beings ourselves.

Finally, the sin of the shadow angels had to do with arrogance and the misuse of knowledge and power. Doesn't this sound familiar as we reflect on the last three centuries of Western civilization? Some amazing knowledge has come forward during this period, and some amazing and healthy empowerment too. But there has also been a dark side. Arrogance has brought about so much of our ecological despair today. The Faust myth is a statement about the misuse of knowledge, power, and arrogance in our effort to know the universe. Do the shadow angels not represent the shadow side of Western civilization, a side that has taken arrogance and the misuse of knowledge and power as a normal way of life?

---

3. Matthew Fox, *Sheer Joy: Conversations with Thomas Aquinas on Creation Spirituality* (San Francisco: HarperSanFrancisco, 1992), 161.

Rupert: I would like to take up your point about the close links of angels to cosmology. The association of angels with the heavens is what came to me first of all. I grew up in Newark-on-Trent, a market town in Nottinghamshire, England, where there's a magnificent medieval parish church. In the roof of the church, as in many late-medieval churches, the beams are supported by carved angels. And in the great Gothic cathedral of Lincoln, only fifteen miles from Newark, there's a part of the cathedral called the angel choir. High up are these angels playing musical instruments—the celestial choirs. To see them you have to look up, so from childhood this is my image of the angels. They are associated with the stars. And this is what I'd like to talk about first, the cosmological aspect of the angels and particularly their association with the heavens.

In the Middle Ages, as in all previous ages, it was generally believed that the heavens were alive, the whole cosmos was alive. The heavens were populated with innumerable conscious beings associated with the stars, the planets, and maybe the spaces in between. When people thought of God in heaven, they were not thinking in terms of some vague metaphor or some psychological state, they were thinking of the sky.

"Our Father, who art in heaven." Nowadays, I suppose, many Christians assume that this is a merely metaphorical statement, nothing to do with the actual sky. The heavens have been handed over to science; the celestial realm is the domain of astronomy. And astronomy has nothing to do with God or spirits or angels; it is concerned with galaxies, the geometry of the gravitational field, the emission spectra of hydrogen atoms, the life cycles of stars, quasars, black holes, and so forth.

But this isn't how people used to think. They thought that the heavens were full of spirits and of God. And indeed if you think of God as omnipresent, everywhere, divinity must be present throughout the whole universe, of which the earth is but an infinitesimal part.

Through the scientific revolution of the seventeenth century, the universe was mechanized, and at the same time the heavens were secularized. They were made up of ordinary matter gliding around in perfect accordance with Newtonian laws. There was no room in them for angelic intentions. Angels have no place in a mechanistic world, except perhaps as psychological phenomena, existing only within our imaginations.

But this mechanistic worldview is now being superseded by science itself. Recent scientific insights are leading us toward a new vision of a living world. This is a key theme of my book *Science Set Free* (called *The Science Delusion* in the UK).

The old mechanical universe was a vast machine, gradually running out of steam as it headed toward a thermodynamic heat death. But since the 1960s it has been replaced by an evolutionary cosmos. The universe began very small and hot in the primal fireball, less than the size of a pinhead, and has been expanding ever since. As it grows, it cools down. More and more structures, forms, and patterns develop within it. At first, there were no atoms, no stars, no galaxies, no elements like iron and carbon, no planets, no biological life. As the universe expanded, all these things came into being somewhere for the first time, and were then repeated countlessly in many places and times. This growing, evolving universe is nothing like a machine. It is more like a developing organism.

Instead of nature being made up of inert atoms, just inert bits of stuff enduring forever, we now have the idea that atoms are complex structures of activity. Matter is now more like a process than a thing. As the philosopher of science Sir Karl Popper has put it, "Through modern physics materialism has transcended itself." Matter is no longer the fundamental explanatory principle but is itself explained in terms of more fundamental principles, namely fields and energy.

Instead of living on an inanimate planet, a misty ball of rock hurtling around the sun in accordance with Newton's laws of motion, we can now think of ourselves as living in Mother Earth. The Gaia hypothesis puts into a contemporary scientific form the ancient intuition that we live in a living world.

Instead of the universe being rigidly determined, with everything proceeding inexorably in accordance with mechanical causality, we have a world to which freedom, openness, and spontaneity have returned. Indeterminism came in through quantum theory in the 1920s. More recently, chaos theory has confirmed that the old ideal of Newtonian determinism was an illusion. Science has been liberated from the idea that we live in a totally predictable and rigidly determined universe.

Instead of nature being uncreative, we now see it as creative. Charles Darwin and Alfred Russel Wallace gave a scientific formulation to the idea that plants and animals are brought forth by Mother Nature herself. But for a long time, physicists denied that evolution had any part to play in the cosmos as a whole. They went on believing that it was an uncreative machine until the 1960s. But we have now come to see that creative evolution is not confined to the realm of biological life; the evolutionary development of the entire cosmos is a vast, creative process.

Instead of the idea that the whole of nature would soon be fully understood in terms of mathematical physics, it turns out that 96 percent of the matter and energy in the cosmos is "dark matter" and "dark energy," utterly unknown to us. It is as if physics has discovered the cosmic unconscious. We don't know what this dark matter and energy is, or what it does, or how it influences the way things happen.

Moreover, the evolutionary cosmology throws the old idea of eternal "laws of nature" into doubt. If nature evolves, why shouldn't the laws of nature evolve as well? How could we possibly know that the "laws" that govern you and me—the crystallization of sugar, the weather, and so on—were all there at the moment of the Big Bang? In an evolutionary universe, it makes more sense to think of the laws

Nested hierarchy of morphic units. The diagram could represent, for example, cells in tissues, in organs, in organisms; or planets in solar systems, in galaxies, in galactic clusters.

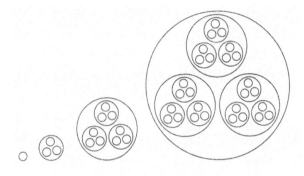

of nature evolving too. I think it makes even better sense to regard the regularities of nature as more like habits. And the habits of nature evolve. Instead of the whole universe being governed by an eternal, mathematical mind, it may depend on an inherent memory. This is the basis of my hypothesis of morphic resonance, memory in nature.[4]

Finally, instead of everything being explained in terms of smaller bits and ultimate particles, we can now think of the universe holistically, organized in a series of levels of organization in a nested hierarchy or holarchy. At each level, things are both wholes and parts. Atoms are wholes consisting of subatomic parts, themselves wholes at a lower level. Molecules are wholes made up of atomic parts; crystals are wholes made up of molecular parts. Likewise, cells within tissues, tissues within organs, organs within organisms, organisms within societies, societies within ecosystems, ecosystems within Gaia, Gaia in the Solar System, the Solar System in the Galaxy, and so on—everywhere there are levels within levels of organization, each system at the same time both a whole made up of parts and a part within a larger whole.

---

4. For an account of this hypothesis, see Rupert Sheldrake, *A New Science of Life: The Hypothesis of Formative Causation* (Tarcher: Los Angeles, 1982) and *The Presence of the Past: Morphic Resonance and the Habits of Nature* (Times Books: New York, 1988), both published by Park Street Press, Rochester, Vermont, 1995.

At each level, the whole is more than the sum of the parts. I suggest that this wholeness depends on what I call a morphic field, an organizing field that underlies the system's structure. Morphic fields are structured by morphic resonance. They have memory within them. Indeed, they are the bearers of the memory inherent in nature.

At each level of organization, morphic fields animate the organisms, giving them their habits and their capacity to organize themselves. In this sense, molecules, stars, and galaxies are alive, not just microbes, plants, and animals. And if they are alive, are they conscious? Do they have minds or intelligences associated with them?

Consider levels of organization such as Gaia, or the solar system, or the galaxy. If the fields that organize them are associated with spirit, intelligence, or a consciousness, then we are talking about superhuman consciousness. If a galaxy has consciousness, spirit, or mind, that mind is going to be inconceivably larger in scope than that of any professor at Harvard or intellectual in Paris.

Matthew: Yes. During the Newtonian-Cartesian industrial age, angels were banished. There's no room for angels in a machine. There wasn't even room for souls in a machine. And not only were angels banished, they were trivialized. Think of Baroque churches built in the seventeenth century, the same century that science and religion split. Religion took the soul, which became more and more introverted and puny, and scientists took the universe. In Baroque architecture, angels became chubby, cute, little babies that you want to pinch. What we need today is angel liberation.

For theologians it became an embarrassment for three hundred years even to mention angels. But angels are mentioned throughout the Bible. In fact, there are legions of angels. Whenever you talk about cosmology, the angels come out.

In the first century, when the Christian scriptures were written, the number-one question going around the Mediterranean basin was: Are the angels our friends or our foes? Everyone believed in angels in

Greece and Rome; they were part of the accepted cosmology. But the question was: Can we trust these invisible forces of the universe that are moving planets and the elements? How trustworthy is the universe?

That's so interesting because in the twentieth century Einstein was once asked, "What's the most important question you can ask in life?" And his answer was, "Is the universe a friendly place or not?" It's the same question. I tell my students that every time you see angels mentioned in the Bible you should think Einstein, because you're dealing with the same issue. It's the ultimate cosmological issue. Can we trust the cosmos? Is the cosmos benign?

In the numerous hymns to the Cosmic Christ in the Bible, there are allusions to the angels (see, for example, Romans 8.38-39; Ephesians 1.20-21; Colossians 1.15-16; Hebrews 1.3-4). The early Christians were responding to this buzz question in the first century: Christ has power over the angels and archangels, the powers and principalities. What are they saying? They're saying, no matter what these invisible forces are doing with the elements of the universe, the smile of God as represented by the Christ means you can relax, be cool. The universe is a friendly place. There is a benign power over the angels: it is the Christ. The Cosmic Christ tradition is set up in the context of angelology because it's set up in terms of cosmology.

Rupert: Even though the heavens have been secularized and mechanized, these questions have not gone away. A spiritual void was created when the religious imagination withdrew from the heavens, and because the scientific imagination is so impoverished, science fiction has risen up to fill the gap. The heavens have been peopled by the fantasies of science fiction writers. Some of these writers are talented and use the heavens as a projection screen for stories of interest and value. But most are banal; they're not up to the job of giving us a real sense of the awe and wonder of the universe. Spaceships shifting into time warps, the evil empire, star wars, space cops, and aliens—these are hardly adequate representations of the cosmic intelligences. Yet science fiction is the main influence on the way most children first think of the heavens. The cosmological void caused by the expulsion and trivialization of the angels has simply been left to science fiction writers and UFO enthusiasts.

What an incredible loss this is! The conventions of science fiction were established in the context of the mechanical universe, before the cosmological revolution of the 1960s, and take little account of what has been discovered since. We now have a vastly expanded view of the heavens, with countless galaxies, quasars, pulsars, black holes, and 15 billion years of cosmic history. I think one of the things we need to do is recover a sense of the life of the heavens so that when we actually look at the stars, when we actually look at the sky, we become aware of this divine presence in the sky and of the intelligences and the life within it.

Matthew: Yes, today we are recovering the sense of the living earth, Gaia, and in many native traditions, Mother Earth, but it is equally important to recover the sense of the life of the sky, and to bring the two together. Jose Hobday, a Seneca woman who teaches with us, says that when native people dance, their knees bend to go into Earth, but their shoulders roll to pick up Father Sky energy, and it is the two energies together that give the whole complement of energy.

We have not only secularized the sky, we have shot our rockets out there and left our debris out there. We are now out there. But the universe is so much vaster and more amazing and constantly expanding than we had ever imagined. And we are not just talking space; we're talking time. We are picking up light from billions of years ago. When we relate to the sky as well as to the earth, we're talking about the resacralization of time as well as space.

Rupert: In the past, people had a sense that what happened on earth was related to what happened in the heavens. This is the tradition that is preserved in a living form today by astrology. But unfortunately, in the seventeenth century astrology split off from astronomy. Astrology gave meaning to the movements of the heavens and their relation to Earth. The planets still bear the names of gods and goddesses, like Mercury, Venus, and Jupiter, who in the Christian world were regarded as angels. These planetary gods, spirits, or angels with their different dispositions and relationships affected life on earth.

In India it's still generally believed that this relationship between the heavens and the earth is of vast importance. When people arrange marriages—and many marriages are still arranged—an astrologer consults the charts of the prospective bride and bridegroom to make sure they're compatible. If they are, the astrologer will then select the time that they should be married. When I first started living in India, I was surprised to receive wedding invitations from Indian friends and colleagues stating, for example, that the marriage of Radha and Krishnan will be celebrated at 3:34 A.M., or some such outlandish time. And although Indians are late for almost everything, they got it right for such an important event. The tying of the knot linking the two together in marriage would happen at the exact moment when their union was in harmony with the heavens.

Elective astrology, choosing the right dates and times for important events, was still practiced in England up until the eighteenth century. And it was even practiced in the White House by President and Mrs. Reagan!

The relation of the heavens and the earth was very important in the old cosmology. But because astrology and astronomy have split apart, astronomers see no meaning in what's happening in the stars; they see no life, intelligence, or consciousness in the heavens. Astrologers see meaning, pattern, and a relationship between what happens in the heavens and what happens on earth, but unfortunately most never look at the sky. I know very few astrologers who can actually identify the stars and planets. Astrology is done from books, or nowadays, from computer programs. I hope someone will soon start giving courses on astronomy for astrologers. I think it is important to bring these two traditions together again.

In many traditional cultures, myths tell of the way that the people are either inspired by or actually come from particular stars. For example, the Dogon in West Africa have a strong relationship with Sirius, the Dog Star. And to my mind it's perfectly possible that by looking at stars and connecting with the intelligence that's there, by forming a direct link to stars and their spirits, some influence or inspiration could pass from the star to the person consciously opening to it. This has certainly been the belief of people through the ages.

The implications of this tradition are staggering. When we look at the stars, we can consider the possibility not only that some may have planets around them with living beings on them, which I think very probable, but also that the very stars themselves may have a kind of life, intelligence, or spirit.

The stars are organized in larger units, galaxies, each of which contains billions of stars and has a galactic nucleus at its center with unknown properties. There are billions of galaxies in the heavens. And there may be a governing intelligence for each galaxy. And galaxies usually come in clusters, which may in turn have an organizing spirit.

Thus there may be hierarchies of organizing intelligences. Galactic clusters include galaxies; galaxies include solar systems; and solar systems include planets. And at each level there's a wholeness, which is included within a higher level of wholeness. So we have many levels of organization, all of which can be thought of as associated with some kind of intelligence or mind.

In the search for extraterrestrial intelligence (SETI), which some scientists like discussing, they usually concentrate on the possibility that intelligent beings on other planets will transmit signals by radio that are mathematically meaningful, such as the sequence of prime numbers, and from these signals we will be able to infer the existence of intelligent beings wishing to communicate with us.[5] But it may be that communication with other forms of intelligence could be far more direct. It may not rely on radio transmissions. It may not need spaceships. It may not depend on UFOs. Direct mental contact with these celestial intelligences may be possible through a kind of telepathy.

Matthew: For me, there's no doubt that previous civilizations that we call indigenous knew much more than we do about communicating over large distances without technology. It's there too in the lore of some of our Western saints who were psychics.

Rupert: And technology may in any case be of very limited use in communicating with intelligences in other parts of the universe. The SETI program, intermittently funded by the U.S. government, shows up these limitations quite clearly. The standard assumption is that the inhabitants of a solitary planet would broadcast radio signals of a mathematically meaningful kind in the hope of finding another intelligent species somewhere in space. This is what astronomer Timothy Ferris calls the lonely-heart scenario: "Lonesome, technically proficient species seeks same. Object: Communication."[6]

Even if we were to receive and recognize such messages from a planet around a nearby star, communication would be very slow. The nearest star is about 4.2 light-years away, so even if we reply immediately, it will take 8.4 years between their sending a message and receiving our reply. Our galaxy is 100,000 light-years across, so it would take 100,000 years for radio messages to pass from one side of the galaxy to another, and 200,000 years before replies could be received. What civilization would have a life span and record-keeping

4. See, for example, Timothy Ferris, *The Mind's Sky: Human Intelligence in a Cosmic Context* (New York: Bantam, 1992).
6. Ferris, *Mind's Sky*, 3 1.

system adequate to communicate over periods such as that? And as for communication with inhabitants of planets in other galaxies, forget it! The nearest regular galaxy to our own, the Andromeda galaxy, is 1.8 million light-years away, so replies will take 3.6 million years to arrive. For galaxies a billion light-years away, replies will take two billion years.

If the transfer of thoughts can happen faster than the speed of light, then the whole question of interstellar and intergalactic communication looks very different, as it does when we broaden our thinking about intelligences elsewhere in the cosmos. Instead of confining our attention to minds of biological organisms, such as ourselves, living in technological civilizations, we can explore the possibility that planets, stars, galaxies, and galactic clusters also have a kind of consciousness. This is where the traditional understanding and experience of cosmic intelligences may be able to help us, and especially the angelology of Dionysius the Areopagite, Hildegard of Bingen, and Thomas Aquinas.

Consider, for example, the possibility that the sun is conscious. This is not a very far-fetched idea, even in terms of the standard materialistic assumptions of orthodox science. Materialists believe that our own mental activity is associated with complex electromagnetic patterns in our brains. These patterns of electromagnetic activity are generally assumed to be the interface between consciousness and the physical activity of our brains. Consciousness is somehow supposed to emerge from these patterns. But the complex electromagnetic patterns in our brains are as nothing compared with the complexity of electromagnetic patterns in the sun.

The sun is a fireball of plasma assumed to be fuelled by nuclear fusion reactions. A plasma is an ionized gas, and it is highly sensitive to electrical and magnetic influences. The sun is the theater of extremely complex, rhythmic patterns of electromagnetic activity, with an underlying cycle about twenty-two years long. About every eleven years the magnetic polarity of the sun reverses: its north magnetic pole switches to the south, or vice versa; after another eleven years, the poles return to their previous positions. These reversals correspond with cycles of sunspot activity, great flares on the surface of the sun. This reversal of polarity is connected with complex harmonic cycles of vibration, swirling resonant patterns of electromagnetic activity.

If people are prepared to admit that our consciousness is associated with these complex electromagnetic patterns, then why shouldn't the sun have a consciousness? The sun may think. Its mental activity may be associated with complex and measurable electromagnetic events both on its surface and deeper within. If there's a connection between our consciousness and complex, dynamic electromagnetic patterns in our brains, there's no reason that I can see for denying the possibility of this connection in other cases and especially on the sun.

If the sun is conscious, why not the other stars too? All the stars may have mental activity, life, and intelligence associated with them. And this is, of course, precisely what was believed in the past—that the stars are the seat of intelligences, and these intelligences are angels.

Matthew: I'm surprised to hear you say this. You are really sticking your neck out. I've never heard you speak of the sun and stars like this before. But ideas like these would have many implications for worship. We need to set our prayer circles in the context of this vast, alive, complex, and amazing universe, for example. Today we have the electronics to do this. To take worship out of the hands of little books and put it into a cosmology again. Then the angels will be present at worship once again.

The angel that has something to do with the incredible intelligence of the sun ought to be there. In our worship, we ought to be awakening the sense of awe—and awe includes terror—with reality. The universe is our home, and everything we're talking about is our home. This is the temple of God, it's God's home.

Angels are so often depicted as light-beings reflecting the luminosity of the divine one. I know you were struck in reading Thomas Aquinas's statement that angels move from one place to another with no time lapse. You said it reminded you of Einstein's thinking about light. What about the idea of angels as photons, light-bearers?

Rupert: When Aquinas discusses how angels move from place to place, his reasoning has extraordinary parallels to both quantum and relativity theories. Angels are quantized; you get a whole angel or none at all; they move as units of action. The only way you can detect their presence is through action; they are quanta of action. And although when they act in one place and then in another, from our point of view time elapses while they are moving, from the point of view of the angel this movement is instantaneous; no time elapses. This is just like Einstein's description of the movement of a photon of light. Although we as external observers can measure the speed of light, from the point of view of the light itself, no time elapses as it is traveling. It doesn't get older. We still have light around from 14 billion years ago, from soon after the Big Bang, in the form of the cosmic microwave background radiation. After all that time, it's still around and still going strong.

So in modern physics there are remarkable parallels to the traditional doctrines about angels, and I think the parallels arise because the same problems are being considered. How does something without mass, without body, but capable of action, move? Angels, according to Aquinas, have no mass, they have no body. And the same goes for photons: they are massless, and you can detect them only by their action.

Matthew: Does that mean that photons are immortal?

Rupert: Yes, as long as they are moving at the speed of light from place to place. But when they act, they are extinguished through their action, so in that sense they come to an end; they pass on their energy as they act. This, I presume, makes them different from angels.

Although there are parallels between modern physics and medieval ideas about angels, the aspect of modern science that raises the most interesting questions is the theory of evolution. In the Middle Ages, nature was regarded as fixed: the cosmos, the earth, and the forms of life upon it were not seen as evolving. In biology, the idea of evolution was first proposed in a scientific form in 1858 by Charles Darwin and Alfred Russel Wallace. In physics, the notion of cosmic evolution became orthodox in the late 1960s as a consequence of the Big Bang theory of the origin of the universe. Now we see everything as evolutionary in nature. This means that there is a continuing creativity in all realms of nature. Is this all a matter of blind chance, as materialists believe? Or are there guiding intelligences at work in the evolutionary process?

As far as I know, one of the first people to explore this possibility was Alfred Russel Wallace. After he and Darwin together published the theory of evolution by natural selection, Darwin went on to develop a gloomy materialism, which now pervades the thinking of neo-Darwinism, the orthodox doctrine of academic biology. All of evolution must have happened by chance and through unconscious laws of nature, and it has no meaning or purpose.

By contrast, Wallace came to the conclusion that evolution involved more than natural selection and was guided by creative intelligences, which he identified with angels. His conception is summarized in the title of his last book, *The World of Life: A Manifestation of Creative Power, Directive Mind and Ultimate Purpose.*[7] We hear a great deal about Darwin today, but we don't hear much about Wallace. I am fascinated that these very different conceptions of evolution were expressed by the two founders of evolutionary theory; they show that evolution can be interpreted in quite different ways. If you are a materialist, evolutionary creativity can only be a matter of

---

7. London: Chapman and Hall, 1911.

blind chance. But if you believe there are other forces or intelligences in the universe, then there are other possible sources of creativity, whether you call them angels or not.

This raises a problem that Aquinas and other medieval thinkers did not and could not deal with, namely, the role of angels in evolution. For example, as new galaxies appear, presumably the appropriate angels that govern the galaxy must come into being with the galaxy, unless all the angels are there, waiting at the moment of the Big Bang for their moment to come.

Matthew: And maybe angels are recycled, like those that hovered over the dinosaurs; they would otherwise have been out of a job for sixty million years.

Rupert: These are questions that were inconceivable in the Middle Ages. Our evolutionary cosmology does not have less room for angels, but vastly more.

Matthew: Yes. I feel very strongly that as a living cosmology comes back, the angels are returning, because they are part of any sound cosmology. Maybe the angels themselves will bring into our culture some of the imagination that we're calling for.

In my book *The Coming of the Cosmic Christ*[8] I coined the term "deep ecumenism." For me, deep ecumenism is going beyond the level of world religions relating to one another in terms of doctrine and theological study papers, and entering more into their mystical traditions and doing prayer and ritual together.

All religious traditions that we know of have something to say about angels, spirits other than human beings. Buck Ghosthorse, a Lakota spiritual teacher, once said to me, "What you Christians call angels, we Indians call spirits." This is common ground on which all our religious traditions can come together today, in deep ecumenism.

---

8. Matthew Fox, *The Coming of the Cosmic Christ* (San Francisco: HarperSan-Francisco, 1988).

Angels are not labeled Buddhist, Muslim, Hindu, Lutheran, Anglican, and Roman Catholic; they are beyond denominationalism.

Clearly, angels will be part of the movement of deep ecumenism. We are living in a moment in history when we as a species have to ask, what do we have in common? The boundaries are melting between cultures and religions. This makes it important to have a serious discussion of our tradition of angels in the West, not out of jingoism but out of knowing our own tradition well enough so that when we encounter angels and spirits from other traditions, we are not put off or threatened by them. Instead, we can look for the common links, the common truths among the traditions.

The shamanistic traditions of the world are particularly important in our search for wisdom today. Indigenous peoples lived and survived for thousands of years amid such travails as wild beasts and inclement weather and ice ages; they had to discover ways of creating community, healing, educating, and learning. There is a tremendous lore here that has almost been lost, but not entirely, and it has everything to do with spirits and with angels. When praying with Native American peoples, I have experienced remnants of it that fill a gap in my own religious experience. Our Celtic ancestors too had a well-developed theology of angels and spirit guardians.

Rupert: Yes. The awareness of nonhuman spirits is fundamental to the religious experience of practically every tradition, maybe from the time we became human. This may be the primordial ground of religious experience. The awareness of spirits comes before the idea of a single God. It's significant that in the Christian, Jewish, and Islamic traditions, as in the Hindu and Buddhist traditions, there is the continuing presence of a multiplicity of spirits. Even in the most monotheistic of faiths, namely Islam, we find no denial of angels. This ancient strand of religious experience is not negated, but rather amplified by the later evolution of religions.

Matthew: Yet we have one moment in human history when these spirits were excommunicated, and that is the last few hundred years, the modern era. This shows what an amazing rupture and perversion has occurred in human consciousness in the last few centuries as we have attempted to divorce ourselves from our relationship to angels and spirits. I think this helps to explain the price we have paid in terms of ecological disaster, war, and greed. Perhaps the ultimate secularization of our relationships is to banish the angels to a place of ridicule or sentimentalism.

Rupert: Or reduce them to mere manifestations of our own psyche. Many modern people would say, "Okay, people experience angels. But these are just figments of their own imagination. Angels do not exist out there; they are subjective, within people's minds."

It's not difficult for people to accept the subjective existence of angels. The big challenge is to recognize the objective existence of nonhuman intelligences, and that's the challenge that faces us now.

Matthew: I also think we should extend deep ecumenism to science itself. What are the implications of today's science for rediscovering the rich, deep, and broad appreciation of angels that we get from the Western tradition as represented by Dionysius, Hildegard, and Aquinas?

Rupert: This is very important, because what science now reveals to us goes far beyond anything that any tradition in the past has been able to glimpse. They didn't have telescopes, or radio telescopes, or a sense of the vastness of the universe that science has opened up, or a knowledge of the variety of heavenly bodies, or the story of cosmic evolution. As we leave the old, machinelike universe and move toward a more organic sense of evolving nature, we need to ask what kinds of consciousness are there in the universe besides our own.

Dionysius The Areopagite

Dionysius lived in the sixth century, probably in Syria. For many centuries he was wrongly identified with Dionysius the Areopagite, converted by St. Paul in Athens (Acts 17.34). He is more correctly called Dionysius the Pseudo-Areopagite, and is also known as Pseudo-Denys. This confusion gave his writings great authority up to the sixteenth century, and his influence on Orthodox and Western theology has been enormous.

Deeply influenced by the Neoplatonic philosopher Proclus (A.D. 411-485), he combines Neoplatonism with Christianity in his four principal books, *The Celestial Hierarchies, Ecclesiastical Hierarchy, Divine Names,* and *Mystical Theology.* It is in his Celestial Hierarchies that he discusses at length the nine orders of angels as mediators from God to humankind, and it is from that book, which has been so influential in Christian angelology, that most of the following passages are taken. He has been called a "moderate Monophysite" in his theology, Monophysitism being the heretical doctrine that denies the human side of Christ at the Incarnation. But at the Lateran Council of A.D. 649 his works were invoked to combat more extreme Monophysite thinkers, and this invocation of his work by a church council also helped embellish the doctrinal authority of his teachings. Because he elaborates at such length on the nine orders of angels that St. Paul only alludes to lightly, his angelology has greatly influenced Christian theology.

The Multiplicity Of Angels

The scriptural tradition respecting the angels gives their number as thousands and thousands and ten thousand times ten thousand, multiplying and repeating the very highest numbers we have, thus clearly showing that the Orders of the Celestial Beings are innumerable for us; so many are the blessed Hosts of the Supermundane Intelligences, wholly surpassing the feeble and limited range of our material numbers.[9]

Matthew: Dionysius is putting his discussion of angels in the context of the vastness of the cosmos and talking about the numbers being innumerable to us. Centuries later Meister Eckhart would say that the angels outnumber the grains of sand on the earth. So what we're talking about here is a vast array, a vast challenge to our imaginations. Go beyond numbers as we know them—just keep adding zeros to get a sense of angelic numbers.

Rupert: Since vast numbers are usually called astronomical, it brings to mind the obvious connection with the stars. We now recognize a cosmos full of innumerable galaxies, each containing billions of stars. When we look at the night sky we see only the stars in our own galaxy, the Milky Way being the main part of it. Insofar as angels are connected with the stars, then this would, literally, give us an astronomical number of angels.

---

9. Dionysius the Areopagite, *The Celestial Hierarchies*, in *Mystical Theology and the Celestial Hierarchies*, trans. the editors of *The Shrine of Wisdom* (Surrey, England: *The Shrine of Wisdom*, 1965), ch. XIV, 60. All citations from Dionysius are from this text unless otherwise indicated.

Matthew: Astronomical numbers and astronomical beings.

Rupert: Yes. And if we also think of angels being connected with all the different kinds of being in nature, then we have to consider the millions of biological species on this earth, and probably on billions of other planets around other stars and in other galaxies. And then these planets themselves are organisms, as is our planet, Gaia. The vast numbers of forms of organization in nature dwarf our imagination, just as Dionysius says the numbers of angels do.

Matthew: It seems appropriate in that context to turn to one of Dionysius's favorite themes, hierarchy. In fact, he seems to have invented the word itself in his book with the title *The Celestial Hierarchies*.

Hierachies, Fields, And Light

Hierarchy is, in my opinion, a holy order and knowledge and activity which, so far as is attainable, participates in the divine likeness, and is lifted up to the illuminations given it from God, and correspondingly towards the imitation of God.

Now the beauty of God, being unific, good, and the source of all perfection, is wholly free from dissimilarity, and bestows its own light upon each according to his merit; and in the most divine mysteries perfects them in accordance with the unchangeable fashioning of those who are being perfected harmoniously to itself.

The aim of hierarchy is the greatest possible assimilation to and union with God, and by taking him as leader in all holy wisdom, to become like him, so far as is permitted, by contemplating intently his most divine beauty. Also it moulds and perfects its participants in the holy image of God like bright and spotless mirrors which receive the ray of the supreme Deity which is the source of light; and being mystically filled with the gift of light, it pours it forth again abundantly, according to the divine law, upon those below itself. For it is not lawful for those who impart or participate in the holy mysteries to overpass the bounds of its sacred laws; nor must they deviate from them if they seek to behold, as far as is allowed, that deific splendour, and to be transformed into the likeness of those divine intelligences.

Therefore he who speaks of hierarchy implies a certain perfectly holy order in the likeness of the first divine beauty, ministering the sacred mystery of its own illuminations in hierarchical order and wisdom, being in due measure conformed to its own principle.

For each of those who is allotted a place in the divine order finds his perfection in being uplifted, according to his capacity, towards the divine likeness; and what is still more divine, he becomes, as the scriptures say, a fellow-worker with God, and shows forth the divine activity revealed as far as possible in himself. For the holy constitution of the hierarchy ordains that some are purified, others purify; some are enlightened, others enlighten; some are perfected, others make perfect; for in this way the divine imitation will fit each one.[10]

Rupert: What Dionysius says here is related to the Neoplatonic conception of emanations from the One, the source from which things flow out. The idea of a chain of being was very important in the ancient world and remained a common theme in literature right up until modern times. There is a source of being and then every grade of being below that, becoming more and more dimmed the farther the descent into matter. That seems to me the Neoplatonic background of Dionysius's thinking. Would you agree?

---

10. Ch. 111, 29, 30.

Matthew: Yes. And I find that difficult to deal with today. The idea of everything emanating from a source is fine; that's certainly the image I get from the creation story today—everything beginning with a tiny pinprick of a fireball. But the idea that beings have to be distant from matter to be spiritual is, I think, one of the great mistakes made by Hellenistic thinking, and it's set us up for all kinds of dualism.

Also I think there's another implication in his language, for example, in his very first sentence, the language of "being lifted up." The idea of pouring out from the top down sets us up to disparage what is below, whether that is the earth we stand on or the lower chakras of our own nature. There are inherent problems in Neoplatonism that I'm uncomfortable with. The coming together of energy in matter and spirit in matter in our century has managed to dispel these misconceptions based on dualism of matter versus spirit.

But the way Dionysius describes hierarchy is interesting—a holy order and knowledge and activity participating in the divine likeness and of course responding toward an imitation of God. That kind of understanding is useful.

It's interesting that his next definition of hierarchy is about the beauty of God. The very first gift that he's alluding to as flowing out from the source is beauty and light. For him beauty is light. And I think that's very wonderful. I think the recovery of the sense of beauty as being another name for the divine is very important today. It's behind the passion for eco-justice, for example. Beauty is one of the great energy sources that we have as individuals, and our experience of beauty is what we share as a species.

Rupert: But isn't there a problem with the image of God as the source of light? It implies that you've got the brightest source at the top, and farther away you get more mixing in with darkness, and the darkness then becomes another Neoplatonic way of conceiving of matter.

Matthew: Exactly.

Rupert: Darkness in this view is not part of the divine; it's a negative principle. If we see darkness and light as polar principles within the divine, then we get a different view. We get a bottom-up as well as a top-down view. We see that the intermingling of light and matter, the flowing down from a bright source, is not entirely negative or a dilution of some primary divine principle.

Matthew: I had that experience when I stayed awake all night in the woods and I realized that the night is not just the absence of the sun; it has its own energy. The darkness moves in. And it has its own energy and its own power, and this is lost in the Neoplatonic view of things. They put down matter, and they put down darkness, and they put down down.

Meister Eckhart says, "Up is down and down is up," and that's much more contemporary. Buckminster Fuller says anyone using the words *up* and *down* is four hundred years out of date because in a curved universe things go in and out but they don't go up and down.

So I think that the notion of climbing Jacob's ladder, the whole archetype of climbing up, can be an escape from *materia*—mater, mother, matter, the earth. This is part of the hierarchical worldview that Neo-platonism takes for granted, and we can't be at home with that today.

It also has profound political implications. For example, in this text itself there's a statement, a footnote, that is quite troubling. It's a quote from Proclus, who was one of the influential Neoplatonic philosophers: "The peculiarity of purity is to keep more excellent natures exempt from such as are subordinate."

That definition of purity is: keep your hands clean from those who are below you. It would certainly feed any temptations to caste consciousness. It endorses the untouchable mentality, and that's again what distinguishes this Neoplatonic philosophy of Proclus, Plotinus, and

Dionysius from the biblical tradition that honors the poorer things of life as being pure in their own right, welcome in the circle of beings in which we all live. Aboriginal people think in terms of the circle of being, not the ladder. So the question arises: Can we shift this archetype of the chain of being to see it more as a circle or a spiral and not as a ladder?

Rupert: I think so. But I also think there is value in the up-and-down imagery. When we look up, we see the sky. Looking up to the heavens is very important. I think that most of us in the modern world don't look up enough. Our gaze is fixed down on the earth and the things of the earth. Almost everything we buy and sell comes from the earth, as well as the money we buy and sell it with. The heavens, the celestial environment, the limitless potentiality of space, the vast variety of celestial beings are simply not in our gaze at all.

Matthew: Are we really looking up or are we looking out? For example, if you get high enough, say on a mountain or from an airplane or a satellite, you know you're looking out, and that's really when the universe gets vast. In other words, we are only looking out in this limited way because our eyes are not on the top of our heads. It's kind of our biological problem that we have to tilt our heads to see some stars. But not always. When there are horizons—I like that word, horizons—we're looking out beyond the earth. And I'm thinking now of what they call big sky in Montana, where you really do feel the horizon out there, you can see the sky just by looking straight ahead. And I remember once in South Dakota coming out of a sweat lodge and the Milky Way was absolutely on fire: you could see all the stars but they ran like a rainbow from flat earth into a curved space all the way to flat earth again.

But, as you say, in cities people are forced to look up more because we've destroyed the horizon. In any case, I couldn't agree more with your basic point, because it's the vastness of the cosmos that we're missing in the way we look.

Rupert: I agree that looking out is a good way to put it. And the best way of looking at the stars is to lie down. Then you can look without straining your neck and you can really appreciate the sky. I imagine that the earliest stargazers were people like shepherds who slept under the sky.

Looking out at the horizon is also an important way. Most megaliths in the ancient world, like Stonehenge, were observatories for viewing the rising and the setting of the celestial bodies against the horizon. These stones divided up the horizon into arcs or regions.

The idea of hierarchy is important in another way. In any holistic worldview—for example, Whitehead's organismic philosophy of nature, or the holistic worldview as it's developing today within science and philosophy—the essence is that at each level of organization the whole is more than the sum of the parts. Nature is composed of a series of different levels, and this is usually called a hierarchy. It's best called a nested hierarchy, because there are levels within levels (see page 14). For example, within a crystal, considered as a whole, you have molecules. And each of the molecules within the crystal is itself a whole made up of atoms, and each atom is an organism of its own with its nucleus and its electrons in orbit around it. And then each nucleus is a whole of its own consisting of neutrons, protons, and forces that hold them together, and so on.

We see these multiple levels of organization everywhere. Our own bodies, for example, are wholes, containing organs, tissues, cells, organelles, and molecules. And we as individual organisms are part of larger systems; we're part of societies, and societies are like an organism at a higher level. And they're within ecosystems. And then there's the planet, Gaia, and then the solar system, which is a kind of organism, then there's the galaxy and then groups of galaxies.

When you look at nature this way, at every level you find a wholeness that is more than the sum of the parts, and this wholeness includes the parts within it. There's no way you can have a planet separate from a solar system; it's got to be part of this larger whole. You can't have solar systems separate from galaxies, as far as we know. It's rather like the way that San Francisco is a city within the United States. The United States is bigger than San Francisco, and the United States in turn is just one part of the American continent.

We're familiar with this pattern of organization in every sense—geographically, in the way that nature's constituted, and even in the way our language is organized, with phonemes in syllables, syllables in words, words in phrases, phrases in sentences. All are nested hierarchies.

Arthur Koestler suggested another word for a nested hierarchy: holarchy. He preferred the word *holarchy* because it got away from the connotation of priestly rule.

The nested hierarchies or holarchies of nature help us make sense of what Dionysius is talking about. We can see the angelic hierarchies in this inclusive sense. For example, some angels could correspond to the angels of galaxies, others to the angels of solar systems, and still others to those of planets. This is actually how the celestial hierarchies were often pictured, in a series of concentric spheres.

Matthew: I think it's also a relationship of three dimensions. If you make it two dimensions on the ladder, then you're stuck with that dominating and domineering motif. But if you see these as spheres within spheres, they're not standing on top of each other giving one and the other orders; they have their own space and their own configuration.

One point I'd like to emphasize in Dionysius's statement on hierarchy is his remark that each being, "according to his capacity," takes part in the divine order and divine likeness and "becomes, as the scriptures say, a fellow-worker with God, and shows forth the divine activity." He says hierarchy is holy order, knowledge, and activity. Activity flows from this participation in beauty, and being a fellow worker with God is, as he says, divine imitation. I think that gives a dynamic dimension to his sense of hierarchy.

I like very much the term "holarchy." We have to come up with other words because the word *hierarchy* has borne so much weight, perhaps far beyond anything Dionysius intended. Political oppression and other things are included in it. Actually I think the best part of the word *hierarchy* is "hier." In English, when most people hear the word *hierarchy*, they think it means high; those who are up high exploiting those below. But of course it doesn't; *hieros* is Greek and it means sacred. It's because we've lost the sense of the sacred in the heavens and on earth that we're in the trouble we're in.

Rupert: I think holarchy is fine, because actually what *hier* means is not just sacred but holy; and "holy" has the same root in English as "whole." Likewise in Greek *holos* means a whole.

Matthew: Another powerful phrase he uses here is "[Divine beauty] moulds and perfects its participants in the holy image of God like bright and spotless mirrors which receive the ray of the supreme Deity which is the source of light."

Hildegard says every creature is a glittering, glistening mirror of divinity. That's the tradition, and it's a wonderful tradition. God looks at us as in a mirror and sees the Godself. We are divine mirrors. And of course mirrors need light. A mirror in the dark is no good as a mirror. Mirrors are needy; they have to receive. This theme of mirrors that he refers to is very common in the mystical tradition; in fact, the term "speculative mysticism" is about mirror mysticism. The Latin word for mirror is *speculum*. Dionysius is saying that things are mirrors of divinity. It's not about speculating and turning mysticism into a philosophical act of rationalization. It's about finding the mirror image in things. Everything mirrors God.

Angels, then, have a special power of mirroring. Maybe it's like the refined mirrors in the Hubble telescope. There's been a leap forward in the human art of making mirrors, and this has been very important for bringing the light into our telescopes and seeing more of the universe. And the mirror is a very wonderful technological invention. I wonder who made the first mirror? I wonder how shocked the people were to look at it.

Rupert: I would have thought that pools of water would have been the first mirrors, as in the myth of Narcissus.

Matthew: Natural mirrors. Maybe the first mirror was carrying a little pool of water around. That's good.

Rupert: To continue with the idea of hierarchy, an important thing about the organization of natural holarchies is that they can be thought of as levels of organization by fields. I call these fields *morphic fields*, the fields that determine the form and organization of the system. We can think of a galaxy as having its field, a solar system as having its field, and a planet as having its field. The levels of inclusive organization are also levels of inclusive fields. Even without my theory of morphic fields, we still have the idea of a galactic gravitational field, of the solar gravitational field that holds the entire solar system together and makes the planets go round the sun, and of the earth's gravitational field holding us all on the earth and causing the moon to orbit the earth. There are also the magnetic fields of the galaxy, the sun, and the earth, and their associated electric fields. Even if we stick to the limited conceptions of fields at present available within science, we see we've got nested hierarchies of fields, or a holarchy of fields.

The same goes for the electromagnetic fields within a crystal: within the crystal field are the molecular fields; within those, the atomic fields, the fields of the electrons, and the atomic nucleus. These are not only electromagnetic fields but quantum-matter fields.

In many ways the modern conception of fields has superseded the traditional conception of souls as invisible organizing entities. Up until the seventeenth century even electricity and magnetism were described in terms of souls, stretching out invisibly beyond the magnet or electrically charged body and capable of acting at a distance.

Fields are a contemporary way of thinking about the invisible organizing principles of nature. Historically, these invisible organizing principles were thought of as souls. The soul of the universe, the *anima mundi*, has been replaced by the gravitational field. The magnetic soul has been replaced by the magnetic field, the electric soul by the electric field. The vegetative souls of plants and animals, the souls organizing the growth of the embryo and the body, have been replaced in modern developmental biology by morphogenetic fields. The animal soul can be replaced by the fields of instinct and behavior, and our mental activity can be understood in terms of mental fields.

Matthew: Getting away from the idea that the soul is in the body, let's just say the body is in the soul. How distant, how near to the horizon can our soul fields roam? In other words, our thoughts, our hopes, our dreams, our passions, our knowledge? In some way, everything we're talking about is encapsulated in our soul field. We can only talk about what we know or imagine we know, and so in many ways our fields, that is, our souls, are growing as we reach to the perimeters of the universe. So there is an awakening of the human field, you might say. We are moving away from the smallness of soul in the pineal gland or cerebral cortex that the modern era gave to soul as the encapsulating dynamic, the consciousness of everything that we can know.

Rupert: I agree. I think our knowledge does reach out from our brains to include that which we perceive, that which we experience, and that which we know. Our mental fields are vastly larger than our brains, and as our conceptions enlarge and extend, as our sense of the cosmos enlarges, our fields become cosmic in scope.

Insofar as we see angels as organized holarchically, perhaps we can see them as associated with angel fields. Angels themselves could be thought of as a particulate manifestation of the activity of these fields, just as photons are a particulate way of thinking about the activity, the energy, carried in electromagnetic fields.

So angelic beings, like quantum beings, may well have a double aspect, a distributed aspect to do with the region of activity with which they're concerned, and manifestations as quanta of activity.

Matthew: Somehow we're talking about photon and field coming together in the light. Angel light.

Rupert: And their traditional role is as interconnectors, as messengers. The very name *angel* comes from this meaning of "messenger." So they're things that link together; and connecting together is what fields do.

Matthew: And as messengers, how appropriate they are returning in our time, since we're rediscovering the habit of the universe known as interconnectivity.

When we conceived of the universe as being disconnected or isolated, the angels had to go on vacation. Their main task is connecting and interconnecting, and there was not much for them to do within the world machine.

I like the idea of the angel as connector. The tradition is that some connect in terms of knowledge and guiding, some in terms of healing, some in terms of defending, some in terms of inspiring. So it makes sense, in a time when we're rediscovering interconnectivity, that these angels who seem to connect one pole of a relation to another are going to have a lot of employment. We should put up a sign: angels needed. There's plenty of work for angels in a period of interconnectivity.

Rupert: And of course interconnectivity within fields is not a one-way process. If I have a big magnet with a strong magnetic field, and I place a smaller magnet nearby, the field of the bigger magnet both influences and is influenced by the field of the smaller magnet. If I move the smaller magnet, this affects the entire field.

Matthew: Now there we have a good analogy for healthy hierarchy or holarchy. There is mutual influence, where the big magnet is not just telling the little magnet what to do, but there's a give and take.

Rupert: Gravity, even according to Newton, works on that principle. All matter attracts all other matter in the universe. There's the idea of a mutual connection there, not just a one-way influence. Following Einstein, we now see this mutual interconnectivity as mediated through gravitational fields, all contained within the gravitational field of the universe, the universal field.

Insofar as we think of whatever affects us as being mediated through messengers or invisible connections, or angels, then something of what's happening to us and what's happening to the world will be conveyed back through the angelic field to more inclusive levels of organization to more inclusive fields of consciousness.

Matthew: The image of fields is so much healthier to me than the basic image we get of a ladder. A field is three-dimensional.

Rupert: Angels operate in fields of activity, coordinating and connecting. Material bodies are mutually exclusive—you can't have two billiard balls in the same place at the same time—but fields can interpenetrate. For example, the room in which we're sitting is filled with the earth's gravitational field, which is why we're not floating in the air. Interpenetrating the gravitational field is the electromagnetic field, through which we see each other, which is also full of radio waves, TV transmissions, cosmic rays, ultraviolet and infrared rays, all sorts of invisible radiations.

These also don't interfere with one another. Radio waves interfere with one another only if they're at the same frequency. But all the radio programs and TV programs in the world can coexist, interpenetrating the same space and not canceling one another out or denying one another. Even if we take only the fields that orthodox science currently recognizes—quantum-matter fields, electromagnetic fields, and gravitational fields—they all interpenetrate. And so the idea of angels as fieldlike allows us to see how they too can interpenetrate.

Matthew: What I like about the word *field* is that it is an everyday word. Field has a sense of space to it. It feels like an invitation to play: one plays in a field. Also, things grow in a field. A field is generative; it is a place of life and activity. It's also about having your feet on the ground. It's matter, it's earth, it's life bubbling up from below. It's an honoring of the lower chakras. I think fields are a wonderfully rich metaphor for bringing angels down to earth, and yet they are three-dimensional. So I want to honor the word *field* in its nonscientific connotation. It too speaks to us of something everyday and something welcoming.

We can also rediscover the meaning of the word *receptive*. In a way, a field is a mirror. It's pulling in the light and converting it into life through photosynthesis and into food. Wonderful things come from fields. Obviously all food comes from fields. Pastures and orchards and romping places and ball games. Gaia is a playing of fields. She invites people to play.

Yesterday, here in London, I was watching football players kicking the ball in Regent's Park, and I had this experience that Gaia is not just land—Gaia is these two-legged creatures with a rubber ball playing on the land. But for all that play you need fields to play in. And what are relationships? What is a marriage but an effort to create a field? What is a home but a field? Children, bringing new beings into the world, and bearing those who die and everything that passes in between. It's living life in fields, fields of interconnectivity.

Rupert: When Faraday first used the word *field* in science, he was using an ordinary English word that had all these implications already built into it. The primary meaning is agricultural field, and this gives rise to the general sense of a field as a region of activity, as in "battlefield," "field of interest," and "field of view." A field is where you do something. To make fields, the first agriculturalists usually had to cut down the trees. Then they grew things in the cleared space. If we stop cultivating fields, if we stop carrying out the activity of agriculture, the fields revert to forest, as in much of New England. Then we have another kind of field, the natural, self-organizing field of the forest.

Participation and Revelation

Wherefore all things share in that providence which streams forth from the superessential deific source of all; for they would not be unless they had come into existence through participation in the essential principle of all things.

All inanimate things participate in It through their being; for the "to be" of all things is the divinity above Being itself, the true life. Living things participate in Its life-giving power above all life; rational things participate in Its self-perfect and pre-eminent perfect wisdom above all reason and intellect.

It is manifest, therefore, that those natures which are around the Godhead have participated of It in manifold ways. On this account the holy ranks of the celestial beings are present with and participate in the divine principle in a degree far surpassing all those things which merely exist, and irrational living creatures, and rational human beings. For moulding themselves intelligibly to the imitation of God, and looking in a supermundane way to the likeness of the supreme deity, and longing to form the intellectual appearance of It, they naturally have more abundant communion with him, and with unremitting activity they tend eternally up the steep, as far as is permitted, through the ardour of their unwearying divine love, and they receive the primal radiance in a pure and immaterial manner, adapting themselves to this in a life wholly intellectual.

Such, therefore, are they who participate first, and in an all-various manner, in Deity, and reveal first, and in many ways, the divine mysteries. Wherefore they, above all, are pre-eminently worthy of the name angel because they first receive the divine light, and through them are transmitted to us the revelations which are above us. ...

Now, if anyone should say that God has shown himself without intermediary to certain holy men, let him know beyond doubt, from the most holy scriptures, that no man has ever seen, nor shall see, the hidden Being of God; but God has shown himself, according to revelations which are fitting to God, to his faithful servants in holy visions adapted to the nature of the seer.

The divine theology, in the fullness of its wisdom, very rightly applies the name *theophany* to that beholding of God which shows the divine likeness, figured in itself as a likeness in form of that which is formless, through the uplifting of those who contemplate to the Divine; inasmuch as a divine light is shed upon the seers through it, and they are initiated into some participation of divine things.

By such divine visions our venerable forefathers were instructed through the mediation of the celestial powers. Is it not told in the holy scriptures that the sacred law was given to Moses by God himself in order to teach us that in it is mirrored the divine and holy law? Furthermore, theology wisely teaches that it was communicated to us by angels, as though the authority of the divine law decreed that the second should be guided to the divine majesty by the first. ... Within each hierarchy there are first, middle, and last ranks and powers, and the higher are initiators and guides of the lower to the divine approach and illumination and union.

I see that the angels, too, were first initiated into the divine mystery of Jesus in his love for man, and through them the gift of that knowledge was bestowed upon us: for the divine Gabriel announced to Zachariah the high-priest that the son who should be born to him through divine grace, when he was bereft of hope, would be a prophet of that Jesus who would manifest the union of the human and divine natures through the ordinance of the good law for the salvation of the world; and he revealed to Mary how of her should be born the divine mystery of the ineffable Incarnation of God.

Another angel taught Joseph that the divine promise made to his forefather David should be perfectly fulfilled. Another brought to the shepherds the glad tidings, as to those purified by quiet withdrawal from the many, and with him a multitude of the heavenly host gave forth to all the dwellers upon earth our often-sung hymn of adoring praise.[11]

Matthew: Participation is one of the important concepts in Dionysius's work, and I think it's still an important word; in fact, it's certainly part of the new paradigm thinking, going from subject-object relationships to participatory relationships. We all participate in the power of the source. All things, even inanimate things, participate in their being. Living things participate in life-giving power. Rational things participate in wisdom. It's interesting that Dionysius says wisdom and not knowledge. Wisdom includes the heart, so it's a very inclusive kind of knowledge.

The natures that are around God participate more fully because they "have more abundant communion" with the Godhead. That's a nice phrase, abundant communion. This is the source of the angels, their abundant communion. They received their primal radiance in a pure manner. They are receptive to light and to radiance. The word *radiance* too is an important word that is carried through in the mystical

---

11. Ch. IV, 32-34.

traditions. The word *doxa* in the Scriptures means glory or radiance. And the *shekina*, the Jewish tradition of the feminine face of God, is a radiant presence of God. It's about the presence. So the question is not about whether God exists, it's about where is the presence. Where is the radiance? Show me the radiance.

Angels were those who first received the divine light, who first felt the radiance, according to Dionysius. And they in turn transmit revelations to us. So it's interesting that he connects revelation to participation and to the reception of light.

He moves on to talk about people experiencing holy visions and theophanies. *Theophany* is a wonderful word for the beholding of the divine. Finally he applies it to the Scriptures and to the Jesus story. The angels initiated the divine mystery of Jesus. There are many examples of angels in the Jesus story: the angel who announced John the Baptist's birth; the angel who announced Jesus' birth; the angel who told Joseph what to do; the angels who appeared to the shepherds before Jesus' birth; and so on. Participation becomes revelation, coming from the place of abundant communion, the Godhead. The presence of angels at these events in Jesus' life are indicators of the honoring of the Cosmic Christ in Jesus, for where angels are, there too are the cosmic forces.

Rupert: I too like the term "participation." It gives a sense of the divine life immanent in all things, in inanimate, living, and rational creatures. It implies not only a movement from the divine into us, but also that we are part of the life of the divine being.

One thing that comes up again and again in these old discussions of angels that is not clear to me is the idea that "they receive the primal radiance in a pure and immaterial manner, adapting themselves to this in a life wholly intellectual." Dionysius was writing from within the Neoplatonic tradition, and his meaning of "wholly intellectual" was very different from ours. Perhaps you could clarify that, because it's obvious he doesn't mean somebody who's only in his or her head.

The word *intellectual* had a larger sense than we usually give it today, is that right?

Matthew: Yes. I think words that come closer to it today would be "a full consciousness." *Theoria* in Greek really meant what we mean by "meditation." So it's bringing heart and head together in a contemplation. But I also have trouble with that, especially in the context where he talks about "a pure and immaterial manner." Again we're back to the Neoplatonic supposition that you have to be immaterial to be pure and an intellectual to be pure and radiant. And I think that here is a source of a lot of our dualistic difficulties in the West.

I don't find this totally redeemable. I think this is really coming out of a culture that is ill at ease with matter and whose whole philosophy supported that. Matter is at the bottom rung of a chain of being and is only tolerated.

Rupert: This Neoplatonic understanding of matter involved a negation of spiritual principles and gave darkness a negative meaning. Then, through the scientific revolution and materialism, matter took on a different meaning. It was the real stuff of things. For the materialist, matter was the foundation of everything and was conceived of as hard and enduring. But its meaning has changed again in the light of modern physics. Matter is made of energy bound within fields, and therefore matter is a structure of activity. The fields themselves are actually immaterial. The electromagnetic field and the gravitational field are not made of matter; rather, as Einstein said, matter is made of fields. Matter is energy bound within fields, more a process than a thing.

Matthew: It's as if we've gone from one end of the pendulum to the other. First matter is the problem and then spirit is the problem. But, as you say, we're coming closer to a midpoint. I think the word *energy* helps a lot. Aquinas defines spirit at one point as the élan, the impulse that's in everything. So spirit is as much a part of matter as it is of nonmatter.

That's another reason why I think the term "field" is so healthy today. It allows us to honor different expressions of energy, sometimes as matter and sometimes as pure relationship. Matter is not a thing in itself; it's relations and rather immaterial.

Rupert: Quite. It's even immaterial in the literal sense. An atom is more than 99.9 percent empty space—or rather, it is full of fields. Electrons, protons, and neutrons are vibratory patterns within these fields, but insofar as they are regarded as particles, they occupy only a tiny part of the space.

"Revelation" is rather a dry term the way it's used by theologians; I like Dionysius's idea of it as an aspect of participation in divine wisdom and activity.

Matthew: Exactly. Again, it's about relationship, participating in life and wisdom. The image that I have is of a fish in water. The water's in the fish and the fish is in the water. This imagery of participation in the divinity, in the source, is quite an affront to theism. It's panentheistic. It's the idea that everything is somehow bathed in the divine and the divine is washing through everything.

Again, it's not about leaving the earth or going up a ladder to find the divine; it's about waking up to the theophany, the beholding of the divine all around us and within. The term "participation" carries that kind of active, dynamic relationship with divinity.

Rupert: Another implication of this passage is that the angels first participate in what's going to happen, and then they help bring it about. For example, he says, "I see that the angels, too, were first initiated into the divine mystery of Jesus in his love for man, and through them the gift of that knowledge was bestowed upon us." There's a sense that the angels are a creative power; they're part of the creative agency through which the development or unfolding or evolution of events happens.

Matthew: The word *revelation* etymologically means to lift the veil, remove the curtain, disclose. It's like a stage show: the curtain's just rising

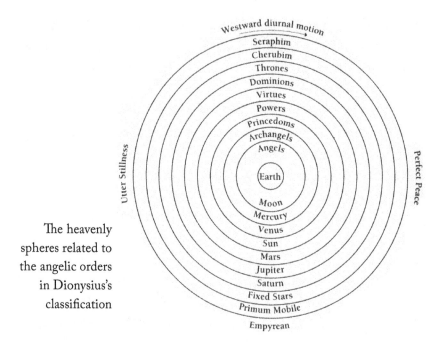

The heavenly spheres related to the angelic orders in Dionysius's classification

and everyone's very excited about this show in which they're about to participate. As you say, the word revelation has been watered down, the energy's been taken out of it, and it's come to mean a handing down of dogma. But really it's about the lifting of veils of illusion and disillusion and projection, to allow reality and beauty and grace to shine through.

The coupling of participation and revelation brings back some of that dynamic character. Anything that's truly revelatory is exciting. It awakens.

THE DIFFERENT KINDS OF ANGELS

The nine choirs of angels, according to the classification of Dionysius:

First Order	Second Order	Third Order
Seraphim	Dominions	Principalities
Cherubim	Virtue	Archangels
Throne	Powers	Angels

The First Order

We are told by Hebrew scholars that the holy name *seraphim* means "those who kindle or make hot," and *cherubim* denotes abundance of knowledge or an outflowing of wisdom. Reasonably, therefore, is this first celestial hierarchy administered by the most transcendent natures, since it occupies a more exalted place than all the others, being immediately present with God; and because of its nearness, to it are brought the first revelations and perfections of God before the rest. Therefore they are named "the glowing ones," "streams of wisdom," "thrones," in illustration of their divine nature.

The name *seraphim* clearly indicates their ceaseless and eternal revolution about divine principles, their heat and keenness, the exuberance of their intense, perpetual, tireless activity, and their elevative and energetic assimilation of those below, kindling them and firing them to their own heat, and wholly purifying them by a burning and all-consuming flame; and by the unhidden, unquenchable, changeless, radiant, and enlightening power, dispelling and destroying the shadows of darkness.

The name cherubim denotes their power and knowing and beholding God, their receptivity to the highest gift of light, their contemplation of the beauty of the Godhead in its first manifestation, and that they are filled by participation in divine wisdom, and bounteously outpour to those below them from their own fount of wisdom.

The name of the most glorious and exalted thrones denotes that which is exempt from and untainted by any base and earthly thing, and the supermundane ascent up the steep. For these have no part in that which is lowest, but dwell in the fullest power, immovably and perfectly established in the most high, and receive the divine immanence above all passion and matter, and manifest God, being attentively open to divine participations. . . .[12]

Therefore the first order of the holy angels possesses above all others the characteristic of fire, and the abundant participation of divine wisdom, and the possession of the highest knowledge of the divine illuminations, and the characteristic of thrones which symbolises openness to the reception of God.[13]

The Second Order

The name given to the holy dominions signifies, I think, a certain unbounded elevation to that which is above, freedom from all that is of the earth, and from all inward inclination to the bondage of discord, a liberal superiority to harsh tyranny, an exemptness from degrading servility and from all that is low: for they are untouched by any inconsistency. They are true lords, perpetually aspiring to true lordship, and to the source of lordship, and they providentially fashion themselves and those below them, as far as possible, into the likeness of true lordship. They do not turn towards vain shadows, but wholly give themselves to that true authority, forever one with the godlike source of lordship.

The name of the holy virtues signifies a certain powerful and unshakable virility welling forth into all their godlike energies; not being weak and feeble for any reception of the divine Illuminations granted to it; mounting upwards in fullness of power to an assimilation with God; never falling away from the divine life through its own weakness, but ascending unwaveringly to the superessential virtue which is the source of virtue: fashioning itself, as far as it may, in virtue; perfectly turned

---

12. Ch. VII, 38-39.
13. Ch. XIII, 57.

towards the source of virtue, and flowing forth providentially to those below it, abundantly filling them with virtue.

The name of the holy powers, co-equal with the divine dominions and virtues, signifies an orderly and unconfined order in the divine receptions, and the regulation of intellectual and supermundane power which never debases its authority by tyrannical force, but is irresistibly urged onward in due order to the Divine. It beneficiently leads those below it, as far as possible, to the supreme power which is the source of power, which it manifests after the manner of angels in the well-ordered ranks of its own authoritative power.[14]

The Third Order

The name of the celestial principalities signifies their godlike princeliness and authoritativeness in an order which is holy and most fitting to the princely powers, and that they are wholly turned towards the Prince of Princes, and lead others in princely fashion, and that they are formed, as far as possible, in the likeness of the source of principality, and reveal its superessential order by the good order of the princely powers.

The choir of the holy archangels is placed in the same threefold order as the celestial principalities; for, as has been said, there is one hierarchy and order which includes these and the angels. But since each hierarchy has first, middle, and last ranks, the holy order of archangels, through its middle position, participates in the two extremes, being joined with the most holy principalities and with the holy angels. ...

For the angels, as we have said, fill up and complete the lowest choir of all the hierarchies of the celestial intelligences since they are the last of the celestial beings possessing the

---

14. Ch. VIII, 43-44.

angelic nature. And they, indeed, are more properly named angels by us than are those of a higher rank because their choir is more directly in contact with manifested and mundane things. ...

Michael is called Lord of the people of Judah, and other angels are assigned to other peoples. ... There is one ruler of all, and to him the angels who minister to each nation lead their followers. ... Pharaoh was shown through visions by the angel who presided over the Egyptians, and the Prince of Babylon was shown by his own angel, the watchful and over-ruling power of Providence. And for those nations the servants of the true God were appointed as leaders, the interpretation of angelic visions having been revealed from God through angels to holy men near to the angels, like Daniel and Joseph. ...

There is one Providence established superessentially above all the invisible and visible powers, and all the angels who preside over the different nations lift up to that Providence, as to their own principle, as far as is in their power, those who willingly follow them.[15]

Matthew: We saw earlier that Dionysius counted an astronomical number of angels, but he also attempts to classify them, categorize them, put them into groups. Dionysius is not the only one to do this. St. Ambrose had a list of nine types of angels; St. Jerome, seven; St. Gregory the Great, nine; St. Isidore of Seville, nine. Moses Maimonides in the Middle Ages had ten; St. John of Damascus had nine; Dante had nine. St. Thomas Aquinas followed the classification of Dionysius.

It seems these efforts to categorize angels are in fact efforts to name the nine spheres of the universe. Seven planets and their domains, thought of as spheres, plus the earth's sphere and the sphere of the fixed stars.

---

15. Ch. XI, 46-49.

This is important because it shows psyche and cosmos coming together. It shows how the ancient wisdom was cosmological. It was not anthropocentric, and it wasn't seeing the soul as being inside the body. I think in picturing these nine spheres we can also think of them as related to the microcosm of the human person, to the chakras. So we have the macrocosm of the celestial spheres and the microcosm of the human spheres. The angels are connectors, administrators, messengers that touch and connect the microcosm, the human being, and integrate us with the spheres of cosmic forces.

Dionysius makes very ecumenical statements about the angels assigned to other nations: how angels guided Pharaoh and the Prince of Babylon as well as the biblical figures of Daniel and Joseph. He calls for a kind of angelic ecumenism when he says that there is only one providence and all the angels serve this one providence.

Rupert: I like the idea of the microcosm and the macrocosm being related, the ordering of our psyches and bodies being related to the ordering of the heavens. This microcosm-macrocosm correspondence helps us to avoid falling into the idea that celestial powers have no relation to us, or falling into the trap of psychological reductionism, regarding all these things as projections of archetypes within the human psyche.

In his rather confusing classification of angels, Dionysius doesn't seem to know quite what to say about dominions, virtues, and powers. He seems to be grasping for distinctive features. The very fact that other people had different classifications shows there was no exact agreement about this. But they needed hierarchies because of the old cosmology, with its series of spheres, one inside the other. They needed to link the angels to the hierarchical order of the heavens as they understood it.

We no longer think in terms of concentric spheres around the earth. We think of different planetary orbits around the sun, with the sun in the Galaxy, and our galaxy within a cluster of galaxies. We now have a much richer and more powerful notion of a celestial hierarchy.

Perhaps the middle hierarchy of angels—dominions, virtues, and powers—could be seen as corresponding to this ordering of the heavens, associated with galactic clusters, galaxies, and solar systems. Perhaps the first hierarchy—seraphim, cherubim, and thrones—are principles lying beyond and within all levels of ordering throughout the cosmos.

The last hierarchy—principalities, archangels, and angels—seems to be more concerned with the ordering of things on earth. It's interesting that each nation was regarded as having its angel, not just the angel of the people but of the place. The angel of Egypt wasn't just the angel of the Egyptian people; it was the angel of the land of Egypt. This fits with the idea found all over the ancient world of tutelary deities, the protectors of each nation and of each land. The Romans recognized them throughout their empire: for example, the guardian spirit of Britain was Britannia, still portrayed on all British paper currency.

The angels protecting the regions of the earth presumably correspond to the principalities, but confusingly, they seem to overlap with the archangels in this role. Michael is the protector of Israel and should be a principality rather than an archangel, according to Dionysius's classification. And then we have the angels that are related to people, such as personal guardian angels.

Dionysius gives us an immensely broad sweep of levels of organization. But his classification is hard to make sense of. The fact that so many angelic taxonomies existed shows that there was confusion over the details. But they agreed on there being many levels of order within the cosmos and on earth.

Matthew: They were rather strapped for details. As you point out, Dionysius's examples get thinner and thinner along the way. But, as you say, maybe our much richer cosmology today gives more scope for filling in the details about fields of organization.

Spirits of the place, spirits of the land—I think that's an important point; angels are not just concerned with people, but with the land itself and all the beings that live on that land and have lived on that land, including the ancestral spirits and the animals.

I like the word *correspondence*; it happens between microcosm and macrocosm, between the great and the local. An angelic ordering as proposed by Dionysius gives us permission to think more in terms of correspondence and less in terms of just being in a box or something. It opens the mind up, opens relationships up.

Rupert: And correspondences are not merely quaint holdovers from a prescientific way of thinking. We have them in modern science. Through the insights of chaos theory and especially through fractal geometry, we see that certain patterns recur at different levels. In self-similar fractals, patterns occur on all scales, however large or small. In the flow of fluids there are the same kinds of vortical patterns in a stirred cup of tea, in whirlpools, in tornadoes, and in the global atmospheric system. We see these spiral patterns in galaxies as well. We can see patterns of a similar kind at all levels of nature.

Likewise, the orbits of the planets around the sun at the astronomical level are reflected in atoms, with the nucleus like the sun and the orbiting electrons like the planets. Magnetic poles exist on all scales, from the atomic level, to compass needles, to the magnetic polarity of the earth and the sun. Science has revealed many kinds of microscopic and macroscopic correspondences. From a holistic point of view, we can see correspondences in the manner in which things are organized at the different holarchic levels of nature.

Matthew: There's something very exciting here. If we go back to his definition of hierarchy and substitute the word pattern, it reads: "Pattern is, in my opinion, a holy order and knowledge and activity . . ."

I wonder if *pattern* might not be a more appropriate and more contemporary naming of hierarchy. We talked about a holarchy, nested levels of wholeness, and wholeness involves pattern. Pattern somehow gets down more to the specific realm, whereas holarchy is the synthesis of it all. Take a developing egg: there's pattern-forming going on inside it. And as you say, corresponding patterns are found in microcosm and macrocosm, in vortical patterns in a stirred cup of tea and in storms on the sun.

Why is it that we're in such a quest for patterns? Maybe that's what the mind is about. It's either making patterns or discovering patterns. Somehow the mind seeks pattern. It is interesting that Erich Jantsch said that "God is the mind of the universe," and the mind evolves. Is that like saying that God is the pattern of the universe, the mind behind the pattern? Our quest for communion with the divine is a quest for communion with the pattern of things. So there's a great joy and great ecstasy in finding patterns. Whether we find them through science or through contemplation, patterns delight us. What is a piece of music, what is a dance? Isn't all art in some way a pattern? Maybe all creativity is an expression of a pattern. Chaos itself, we're learning, differs from order only because it has a more subtle pattern to it.

Rupert: Pattern is clearly to do with form and order, and that's something that fields give to nature. Fields give form, order, and pattern to things. We could say that the patterning aspect of the divine, reflected in nature, corresponds to the Logos principle in the Holy Trinity. This patterning activity is what Dionysius sees the cherubim as imparting: they are to do with knowledge, wisdom, and order. The seraphim are to do with light and burning, with energy. They are therefore the transmitters of the dynamical aspect of the Holy Trinity, the Holy Spirit, corresponding with wind, breath, life, light, movement, inspiration.

In modern science, we have fields, which give patterns, and energy, which gives actuality, movement, and activity. Dionysius sees the cherubim as the patterning or wisdom aspect and the seraphim as the burning or kindling aspect of the first principles underlying the manifested world.

Matthew: It's interesting that the seraphim come first, the Eros, the fire, the energy. This corresponds to the first chakra. And you have that in the first story in Genesis too: the ordering principle comes after there's already energy going on, disorder. In light of what you're talking about, it's interesting to look again at how he describes seraphim in terms of "ceaseless and eternal revolution, ... heat and keenness, the exuberance of their intense, perpetual, tireless activity, ... firing ... unquenchable, changeless, radiant, and enlightening power, dispelling and destroying the shadows of darkness."

That's an incredible description of energy, isn't it? But it's interesting that wisdom in the Jewish tradition is not identified just with Logos; in fact, it's really distinct from it. It is Eros. As the book of Wisdom says, "This is wisdom, to love life." Not just to know about it, but to love it.

Wisdom brings together Logos and Eros, the pattern and the energy. By itself Logos might become knowledge, but together I think they bring about wisdom.

Light and Fire

There is, therefore, one source of light for everything which is illuminated, namely, God, who by his nature, truly and rightly, is the essence of light, and cause of being and of vision. But it is ordained that in imitation of God each of the higher ranks of beings is the source in turn for the one which follows it; since the divine rays are passed through it to the other. Therefore the beings of all the angelic ranks naturally consider the highest order of the celestial intelligences as the source, after God, of all holy knowledge and imitation of God, because through them the light of the supreme God is imparted to all and to us. On this account they refer all holy works, in imitation of God, to God as the ultimate cause, but to the first divine intelligences as the first regulators and transmitters of divine energies.

The lower orders of the celestial beings participate also in these fiery, wise, and God-receptive powers, but in a lower degree, and as looking to those above them who, being thought worthy of the primary imitation of God, uplift them, as far as possible, into the likeness of God. ....[16]

We must ask in the first explanation of the forms, why the Word of God prefers the sacred symbol of fire almost above all others. For you will find that it is used not only under the figure of fiery wheels, but also of living creatures of fire, and of men flashing like lightning who heap live coals of fire about the heavenly beings, and of irresistibly rushing rivers of flame. Also it says that the thrones are of fire, and it shows from their name that the most exalted seraphim themselves are burning with fire, assigning to them the qualities and forces of fire; and throughout, above and below, it gives the highest preference to the symbol of fire.

Therefore I think that this image of fire signifies the perfect conformity to God of the celestial intelligences. For the holy prophets frequently liken that which is superessential and formless to fire which (if it may lawfully be said) possesses many resemblances as in visible things to the divine reality. For the sensible fire is in some manner in everything, and pervades all things without mingling with them, and is exempt from all things and, although wholly bright, yet lies essentially hidden and unknown when not in contact with any substance on which it

---

16. Ch. XIII, 56-57.

can exert its own energy. It is irresistible and invisible, having absolute rule over all things, bringing under its own power all things in which it subsists. It has transforming power, and imparts itself in some measure to everything near it. It revives all things by its revivifying heat, and illuminates them all with its resplendent brightness. It is insuperable and pure, possessing separative power, but itself changeless, uplifting, penetrative, high, not held back by any servile baseness, ever-moving, self-moved, moving other things. It comprehends, but is incomprehensible, unindigent, mysteriously increasing itself and showing forth its majesty according to the nature of the substance receiving it, powerful, mighty, invisibly present to all things. When not thought of, it seems not to exist, but suddenly enkindles its light in the way proper to its nature by friction, as though seeking to do so, uncontrollably flying upwards without diminishing its all-blessed self giving.

Thus many properties of fire may be found which symbolize through sensible images the Divine activities. Knowing this, those wise in the things of God have portrayed the celestial beings under the figure of fire, thus proclaiming their likeness to the Divine, and their imitation of him in the measure of their power.[17]

We must now consider the representations of the celestial beings in connection with rivers and wheels and chariots. The rivers of flame denote those divine channels which fill them with super-abundant and eternally out-pouring streams and nourish their life-giving prolificness.

The chariots symbolize the conjoined fellowship of those of the same order; the winged wheels, ever moving onward, never turning back or going aside, denote the power of their progressive energy on a straight and direct path in which all their intellectual

---

17. Ch. XIV, 62-63.

revolutions are supermundanely guided upon that straight and unswerving course.[18]

Rupert: These are wonderful passages about the primal nature of light and fire and the importance of light and fire as divine images in the Bible and in tradition. The same imagery comes in many different forms. In the Hindu tradition, Shiva, as creator and destroyer, is portrayed as Nataraja dancing in a ring of fire. Fire as purifier, transformer, and also as destroyer is a primal image, found all over the world. We all depend on the sun, which is fire, and all human cultures depend on the domestication of fire. The use of fire is unique to human beings. Fire has played a central role in making us human, and provides a powerful source of images for all people everywhere.

This central role of fire is expressed extraordinarily clearly and beautifully in these passages. The seraphim, the fiery ones, come first. And in the creation story in Genesis, the first creative act of God is to say, "Let there be light," and there is a separation of light from darkness.

Dionysius's imagery of primal light and fire is paralleled in many cultures, and indeed in modern science itself. When people are trying to express this primal, creative event, either they use the name Big Bang, a primary explosion in the intensest conceivable heat, or they use phrases such as "the primal fireball." Modern cosmogony starts with this inconceivable heat or fire, from which all things come into being.

In the passage about the rivers and wheels and chariots, Dionysius talks about "winged wheels, ever moving onward." This image gives us a combination of movement in a line and movement in cycles. Mathematically, this combination of onward movement and cycles is represented in wave equations. The physics of waves, on which almost all of modern physics is grounded, is based on the mathematics of

---

18. Ch. XIV, 67.

revolution of the wheel. The sine wave is what you get when you stretch out an algebraic model of the rotation of the wheel.

Matthew: Chakras are represented by rotating wheels, and in East and West the chakras correspond to the heavenly spheres. The first chakra is the chakra of fire, which, as you pointed out, is oscillating and vibratory. But it is also the seed of the Kundalini, the fire that lights a fire to all the other chakra points.

It is telling how other traditions celebrate the fire, and certainly fire is very important for Dionysius's worldview. He talks about the reception of the "source of light," "the ray of the supreme deity" that we are mystically filled with. Time and again he identifies the experience of beauty with the experience of light.

I think part of his preference for this image of fire and light may come from his living in the desert. This is a Syrian desert monk, so he must have learned to befriend fire and light on a daily basis.

He speaks of the divine radiance, of our receiving light and the essence of divinity as light. There's one source of light for everything that is illuminated. That word alone, *illumination*, our becoming enlightened, is obviously not restricted to the West or the Middle East but is obviously a Buddhist idea too, the breakthrough into the light.

He says that we participate in the divine ray. Again this takes me back to the Hebrew tradition of *shekina*, which is radiance: the divine fire, the presence of the fire, Moses experiencing God in the burning bush, and the fire that accompanied the people of Israel in traversing the desert. Dionysius says that in the Scriptures, "the Word of God prefers the sacred symbol of fire almost above all others ... this image of fire signifies the perfect conformity to God of the celestial intelligences."

He's really connecting to the fire of waves and photons when he says fire is "in some manner in everything, and pervades all things without mingling with them." That's interesting that fire doesn't give itself away; it's "exempt from all things and, although wholly bright,

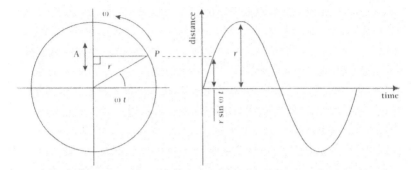

Sine wave, and its mathematical relationship to circular motion. The point P moves around the circle at a constant speed, represented by the angular velocity ω. The up-and-down movement of A plotted against time is called a sine wave because the equation describing this motion involves the sine of the angle ω.

yet lies essentially hidden and unknown … irresistible and invisible." It heats, it revives, it illuminates, it transforms, and it comprehends. "It seems not to exist, but suddenly enkindles its light." I'm thinking of a fire that appears to go out, and you put some paper on it and it comes to life again. That's why he says that wise people "have portrayed the celestial beings under the figure of fire," because fire is one of the richest metaphors for divinity itself.

You could talk about fire in each of the chakras, for there is a fire element in all of them. The sexual fire in the second chakra; the angry fire, the passion of anger, in the third chakra; the fire of warmth in the heart that melts—"the first effective love is melting," as Aquinas says; the fire of the throat, the prophetic voice that speaks out; the fire of intuition, illumination, and creativity in the third eye. And then the fire of the top chakra, the crown chakra, connects to all the other fires in the universe, including the angelic fires, the celestial beings.

Rupert: Whereas Dionysius talks about fire hidden in all things, science talks about energy. There's heat in all things, and it's only at absolute zero, the theoretical limit, that this vibratory thermal energy ceases. But even then, there is still the hidden energy that holds chemical bonds together, and the energy that's combined in atomic and subatomic matter that's bound in matter by fields.

As the quantum physicist David Bohm said, "Matter is frozen light." Light energy can be trapped in material form, in the vibratory nature of atoms and subatomic particles. And matter can give out light again. For example, in burning paper, the energy released originally came from the sun, and was trapped in the leaves of trees through photosynthesis, and hidden in wood.

The principles of thermodynamics, enunciated in the nineteenth century, are a great unificatory insight of science. What they show is that all forms of energy can be transformed to all others, and in the heart of all things is energy. The most visible and explicit form of energy is fire, but energy is hidden in all things. The primal source of all this energy, according to modern cosmology, is the original fireball through which the universe was born.

Matthew: It's interesting that one of the great sins of the spirit is inertia. What is inertia? Lack of energy, lack of fire. And Hildegard of Bingen says, "Why do you live without passion, why do you live without blood?" In other words, where is the fire?

Pentecost, a breakthrough of the spirit, comes again in the imagery of fire. The fire that melts, the fire that inspires, the fire that transforms. As you say, fire is an everyday event because photosynthesis is literally the process of converting light to food. So we eat fire when we eat food.

I remember when my dog died, just putting my hand near his body I knew it was not him because the warmth had gone. Life and warmth go together.

Once I prayed in a kiva with a Hopi Indian, and we talked about praying with rattlesnakes. I asked him, "When you capture a snake and start praying with it, isn't it very nervous?" He said, "Yes, it is, but I sing to it. A snake is very sensitive to cold and heat, being a reptile, and it catches the heat of the song and calms down quickly." The idea that music and heart-work can create warmth is another generator of fire and energy. Perhaps it's as potentially powerful as photosynthesis. But we haven't yet discovered how to unleash our warmth.

And Hildegard says, "No warmth is lost in the universe."

Angels as Gods

You will find, moreover, that the Word of God not only calls these celestial beings above us gods, but also gives this name to saintly men amongst us, and to those men who, in the highest degree, are lovers of God; although the first and unmanifest God superessentially transcends all things, being enthroned above all, and therefore none of the beings or things which are can truly be said to be wholly like him, save in so far as those intellectual and rational beings who are wholly turned towards union with him, as far as is in their power, and who, uplifting themselves perpetually, as far as possible, to the divine radiance, in the imitation of God (if it be lawful so to speak) with all their powers, are thought worthy of the same divine name.[19]

Rupert: The idea of celestial beings as gods enables the angels in Christianity, Islam, and Judaism to be related to the *devas* of Hinduism, known as "the shining ones," and to the gods of many other religions. Dionysius explicitly recognized the protecting gods of Egypt and Babylon as angelic (see page 54).

The gods in polytheistic religions are assimilated into monotheism by being treated as angels. If the many gods are recognized as subject to the one supreme God, they can be accepted as divine intermediaries

---

19. Ch. XII, 53-54.

and as divine powers. The difference between monotheism and polytheism, at first sight so stark, is softened and modified by the recognition of the angels.

Matthew: That's very interesting. It certainly shows a deep, ecumenical attitude on the part of Dionysius, and one wonders if the acceptance of celestial beings as gods would also apply to celestial beings as goddesses, an opening to the feminine deities as well as to the masculine ones.

In 1 Corinthians 8.5, there's a rather unusual and unexpected statement by St. Paul that confirms what you were talking about: "Even though there be so-called gods, whether in heaven or on earth—and indeed there are many such gods and many such lords—yet for us there is one God, the Father, from whom are all things, and we exist for him. There is one Lord, Jesus Christ, through whom are all things, and we exist through him."

This passage is very like the Cosmic Christ passages throughout the New Testament about the Christ having power over the angels, archangels, thrones, and dominions. St. Paul is making a lot of space for invisible forces and powers, but he is also establishing that there's no need to be anxious about these powers because the Christ, representing God the creator, has power over all of them. Part of the good news is that the cosmos in which we are immersed is essentially a friendly place, because God the creator and the Christ have the last word over what these gods or angels are busy doing.

It is striking that Dionysius in this passage says that there are beings trying to imitate God who are thought worthy of the same divine name. He also uses the term "divinization." What the West calls our sanctification, the East calls our divinization: it is about the Christ-nature, the God-nature, in all of us. It is a pity how seldom Western theologians use the term or even the concept. Meister Eckhart is an exception to this rule, however.

Angels in Nature

The plenitude of the infinite power of God in harmonious rhythmic measure fills all things. ... From it are the Godlike powers of the angelic orders; from it they have their unchangeable being and all their intellectual and immortal perpetual activities; and their own stability and unfailing aspiration to the good they have received from that infinitely good power which itself imparts to them their power and their being and their perpetual aspiration to Being, and the power to aspire to that ceaseless power.

From this ever-flowing power men and animals and plants and the entire nature of the universe are filled; it disposes unified natures to mutual harmony and communion and gives to each individual thing the power to be according to its own particular reason and form, distinct from and unmingled with others. And it guides according to their appropriate good the laws of the universe and the activities related to them, and guards the immortal lives of the individual angels inviolate, and keeps the heavenly and luminous and starry substances unchanged in their own orders, and gives eternity the power to be and differentiates the cycles of time in their beginnings and joins them together in their returning, and it makes the powers of fire unquenchable and the flow of water unfailing. It sets a bound to the fluid air and establishes the earth upon the void and maintains its imperishable and life-bearing travail. It preserves the mutual harmony of the mingling elements unconfused and yet inseparable, and makes fast the bond uniting soul and body. It quickens the powers of growth and nourishment in plants and supports the essential powers of the whole and protects the stability of the universe from dissolution, and bestows even deification itself by giving the capacity for this to those who are being deified. And, in a word, there is no single thing in the entire universe which is outside the almighty embrace and safe-keeping of the divine power. For that which is absolutely without power has no existence or qualities and no place whatever in the universe.[20]

The name winds given to the angels denotes their swift operations and their almost immediate impenetration of everything, and a transmitting power in all realms, reaching from the above to the below, and from the depths to the heights, and the power which uplifts the second natures to the height above them, and moves the first to a participative and providential upliftment of the lower.

But perhaps it may be said that the name winds, applied to the aerial spirit, signifies the divine likeness in the celestial beings. For the figure is a true image and type of divine energy corresponding to the moving and generative forces of Nature, and a swift and irresistible advance, and the mystery, unknown and unseen by us, of the motive principles and ends. For he says: "Thou knowest not whence it cometh nor whither it goeth." The scriptures also depict them as a cloud, showing by this that these holy intelligences are filled in a supermundane manner with the hidden light, receiving that first revelation without undue glorying, and transmitting it with abundant brightness to the lower orders as a secondary, proportionate illumination; and further, that they possess generating, lifegiving, increasing, and perfecting powers by reason of their intelligible outpourings, as of showers quickening the receptive womb of earth by fertilizing rains for life-giving travail. ...[21]

Let us pass on to the sacred unfoldment of the symbolism which depicts the celestial intelligences in the likeness of beasts.

---

20. Dionysius the Areopagite, *The Divine Names*, trans. the editors of *The Shrine of Wisdom* (Surrey, England: The Shrine of Wisdom, 1957), ch. VIII, 69-70,nn.1,5.
21. *Celestial Hierarchies*, ch. XV, 65.

The form of a lion must be regarded as typifying their power of sovereignty, strength, and indomitableness, and the ardent striving upward with all their powers to that most hidden, ineffable, mysterious divine unity. ...

The figure of the ox signifies strength and vigour and the opening of the intellectual furrows to the reception of fertilizing showers; and the horns signify the guarding and unconquerable power. The form of the eagle signifies royalty and high soaring and swiftness of flight and the eager seizing of that food which renews their strength, discretion, and ease of movement and skill, with strong intensity of vision which has the power to gaze unhindered, directly and unflinchingly upon the full and brilliant splendour of the brightness of the divine Sun.

The symbolism of horses represents obedience and tractability. The shining white horses denote clear truth and that which is perfectly assimilated to the divine light; the dark, that which is hidden and secret; the red, fiery might and energy; the dappled black and white, that power which traverses all and connects the extremes, providentially and with perfecting power uniting the highest to the lowest and the lowest to the highest.

If we had not to bear in mind the length of our discourse, we might well describe the symbolic relations of the particular characteristics of animals already given, and all their bodily forms, with the powers of the celestial intelligences according to dissimilar similitudes: for example, their fury of anger represents an intellectual power of resistance of which anger is the last and faintest echo; their desire symbolizes the divine love; and in short, we might find in all the irrational tendencies and many parts of irrational creatures, figures of the immaterial conceptions and single powers of the celestial beings.[22]

---

22. Ch. XV, 66-67.

Matthew: In these passage we have a redemption of the word "power." The angelic orders receive their godlike powers, including their aspiration to goodness, from an infinitely good power. Dionysius celebrates their power to aspire to that ceaseless power.

But this power is not limited to the angels. It's the same power that flows into men, animals, plants, and the "entire nature of the universe." All things are filled with this ever-flowing power. It's interesting that all beings, including angels, participate in this same energy or power. From this point of view, we are not different from the angels. Dionysius offers the image of power as a maternal embracing—one that extends great security: "There is no single thing in the entire universe which is outside the almighty embrace and safe-keeping of the divine power."

The universe is filled with power. Every wind is a power, from all directions. All beings share in the angelic powers, and angels penetrate everything. I like the phrase "reaching from the above to the below, and from the depths to the heights." And the angels possess generating, life-giving powers. He sees powers everywhere in nature in which angels play, including characteristics of the animals such as fury and anger. That's interesting because elsewhere he insists on the intellectualization of these immaterial spirits. Here he seems to be attributing anger, resistance, and desire—in other words, passions—to the angels.

It seems that nature and angels come together for him at the level of power. Maybe we have other names for that, like energy or force. But he has a very cosmic sense of the omnipresence of the divine power expressing itself through angels and all other creatures. The divine power is playing in all these fields. It's all one power but it's playing in different forms, including the angelic species.

Rupert: Yes. He seems to imply that each kind of organization in nature, including light and fire, wind, and the life of animals, is perfused with consciousness; not an undifferentiated or transcendent divine consciousness, but a differentiated consciousness appropriate to each kind of organization.

Nature is organized by fields, and these fields are the realms of activity that bind and order the energy or power. If divine power flows through and into all things, if it is the energy of all things, and if it is channeled through the angels, then the fields that give this power its differentiated forms are associated with consciousness and intelligence. The angels are, as it were, the consciousness of the fields operating at all levels of nature, as in the flow of the winds and in the powers of living beings such as animals. The generative powers of nature are associated with intelligence.

Dionysius gives us a view of living nature pervaded by differentiated intelligence, by consciousness, participating in the divine being.

Matthew: Would you say this is animism?

Rupert: More than animism. Animism says that nature is alive and that all living beings are pervaded by souls. But souls needn't necessarily be conscious. The soul of a plant, and even the vegetative psyche that organizes the growth of a human embryo, is not necessarily conscious. Most soul or psychic activities are unconscious or habitual. Even in our own case, the great majority of our psyche is unconscious.

What he's saying goes beyond animism. He is not simply saying that all nature is alive and that there are animating souls in all nature. If we think in terms of fields instead of souls, his doctrines imply not only that all things have power or energy organized by fields, but that they participate in consciousness and intelligence through the angels, and indeed through the angels participate in the divine nature. Their energy and power are also participations in the divine nature, mediated through the angelic hierarchies not as a blind communication of force, but always guided by intelligence.

I think this view is particularly relevant in the modern context, even more so than at the time of Dionysius when nature was considered to be fixed—the species of animals didn't change; there was no evolution in nature.

We now see everything in an evolutionary context. The intelligences associated with all levels of organization could be seen as playing a creative or guiding role in the evolutionary process.

Matthew: I'd say it takes more intelligence to carry on creation as a process than just to make it happen all at once.

Rupert: So these doctrines of angelic intelligences take on an extraordinary new relevance in the light of evolutionary cosmology.

Matthew: This recalls what Erich Jantsch said: God is the mind of the universe, which evolves and creates self-organizing systems or fields. It underscores the immanence of the divine mind and purpose —and therefore love—within the many, many fields in which we live, move, and have our being.

★ ★ ★

St. Thomas Aquinas

St. Thomas Aquinas (1225-1274) is recognized as an intellectual genius whose powers of theological synthesis were matched by his depth of soul and feeling. At the age of five he was sent by his family to the Benedictine abbey of Monte Cassino with hopes that he might become abbot someday. He disappointed his family when he attended the University of Naples as a teenager and expressed an interest in becoming a Dominican. Eventually that dream came about, and after studying with Albert the Great in Cologne, he became Master of Theology at the University of Paris.

The volume and quality of his writings is immense, filling as they do twenty-six encyclopedia-size volumes as he attempted to reinterpret Christianity in light of the new cosmology of his era, that of Aristotle, the fifth-century-B.C. Greek philosopher. This provoked controversy both from the Augustinian-based fundamentalists in the church and from the left-wing Aristotelians who sought an atheistic version of Aristotle. Thus Aquinas's life was characterized by immense struggle and controversy and culminated in his being rendered mute his last year. The only thing he said was: "All I have written is straw."

Aquinas synthesizes centuries of traditional thought about angels while contributing new layers of questions and insights to the topic of angelology. His influence on the history of theology has been very great, and one of the titles he has been given is "Doctor Angelicus," or Angelic Doctor.

Angels and the Cosmos

The entire corporeal world is governed by God through the angels.[23] The angels are part of the universe in the sense that they do not constitute a universe on their own but are combined with the physical creation to form one, total world. This, at any rate, seems a likely inference from the relationship of creature to creature. For the total good of the universe consists of the inter-relationship of things and no part is complete and perfect in isolation from the whole.[24]

Rupert: Aquinas gives us a vision of the universe under the guidance of intelligence and consciousness, a very different picture from the inanimate and unconscious world portrayed by mechanistic science.

Matthew: And he emphasizes the omnipresence of the angels—that angels are everywhere, wherever there's providential government to be exercised. This means that angels can be operating in small, individual situations, as in the tradition of guardian angels, or in terms of nations, continents, planets, solar systems, and galactic systems.

Rupert: In this context, our modern understanding of the cosmos as evolutionary would mean that the whole evolutionary process is governed by the angels. This would go far beyond the idea held in Aquinas's time that God created everything together with the angels in the beginning. Then the angels governed what was there.

---

23. *Summa Theologiae* (ST) 1, q. 63, a. 7.
24. ST 1, q. 61, a. 3.

Now we have the idea of a creative process extended throughout the entire history of the universe and still going on today.

We also have a much greater sense of the vastness of the cosmos, containing billions of galaxies and uncountable trillions of stars. So this statement, "the total good of the universe consists of the inter-relationship of things and no part is complete and perfect in isolation from the whole," taken in a modern context, greatly enlarges the scope, activity, and power of the angels.

Matthew: And it gives a new relevance to this wonderful statement about the interconnectivity and interrelationship throughout the universe, that angels are not out on their own, either running things or dipped in bliss, but they're part of a larger community. There's one total world, one cosmos, one community that they are a rich part of.

This cosmology helps explain why angels have been ridiculed during the machine era when the principle of interrelationship was not honored. Now, given a universe based on the interrelationship of all things, there is a real place for angels. And consciousness among angels includes not just awareness and knowledge but also love. If angels are everywhere, then will and loving presence are also everywhere.

Joy and Wholeness

A thing can be useful ... as a part in a whole; and it is in this way that the services done by blessed angels are of use to them. They are a part of their joy itself: for to share with others from one's own fullness is of the very nature of fullness.[25]

Matthew: The angels are not just busy little bees performing some kind of duty in the universe. They are involved in this amazing, creative process of the unfolding of the universe from a fireball to

---

25. ST 1, q. 62, a. 9, ad. 2.

being one trillion galaxies and growing. So you can imagine how their intelligences and their creativity are challenged in carrying on this glorious work of being instruments of providence to behold and assist the unfolding of the universe in its immense complexity and simplicity.

And they're taking joy in this. We too take joy at expressing order within the chaos of things so that beauty and glory truly express themselves. To share one's joy is one of the great felicities of living.

Rupert: The creative process in nature is always one of the creation of new forms, new patterns that have an inherent wholeness. The creative process involves jumps or leaps to new levels of synthesis; it doesn't give rise to half a galaxy, or half a sun, or half an idea. Here there is a connection between wholeness and fullness, from which joy comes.

Matthew: And that's exactly how Aquinas puts it in this very passage; he talks about being part of the whole. And as part of the whole, the service done by the angels is of use to them and of joy to them. Cosmology and community go together. We work to be part of a whole.

Angels are part of the great work of the unfolding universe. In this regard angels can lead human beings into the important question: Are we part of the great work? Are we connected to the whole?

Angels and the Heavens

The place of the angels in the scale of spiritual being corresponds to that of the heavenly bodies in the corporeal world; thus Dionysius calls them heavenly minds.[26] Isaiah talks about an army of celestial wonders such as the heavens, the stars, and angels.[27]

---

26. ST 1, q. 58, a. 3.
27. Cited in Matthew Fox, *Sheer Joy: Conversations with Thomas Aquinas on Creation Spirituality* (San Francisco: HarperSanFrancisco, 1992), 185.

Rupert: Here Aquinas makes explicit the connection of the angels with the heavens, the celestial nature of the angels. A lot of the literature and discussion of angels in recent years has been concerned with guardian angels, which help us out and guide us. But such guardians of human beings are a tiny part of the creative intelligence in the cosmos when we take into account the role of the angels in galaxies, in stars, and in the entire process of cosmic evolution. If we just look at most modern books on angel helpers, we can easily forget that we are dealing with orders of beings of vast cosmological importance and scope.

Matthew: Yes, it's part of our human arrogance to think that the angels' only job is to sit on our shoulders or to usher our children around.

People who think dualistically about religion usually think of heaven as being another place after death. But what's being integrated here is the mystery and the vastness of the universe itself; angels have a governing role in this vast temple in which we dwell, the temple of the spirit that is the universe itself.

Rupert: Modern science itself is based on the idea that the universe is governed by invisible principles, the laws of nature. These laws are essentially intellectual because mathematical equations are things that exist in minds. They're not physical things you actually encounter in the world. You don't look through an electron microscope and see Schrodinger's equation among the molecules, or look through a telescope and see Einstein's equations written in the sky. They are invisible governing principles. But they are conceived of in an extremely limited and noncreative sense, as abstract mathematical equations rather than as living minds with creative power. Creativity is supposed to come into the evolutionary process through blind chance.

Matthew: These laws are truly disembodied, aren't they?

Rupert: They're totally disembodied. The idea that the universe is governed by disembodied intelligence is the standard modern view. It's just that we've produced an extremely arid, limited, narrow version of it.

Matthew: Without love, and without *joy*.

Rupert: Yes. And insofar as people believe that mathematical equations are the ultimate truth, this is a form of idolatry. It treats manmade mathematical models as the ultimate reality.

In an evolving universe, it seems to me that the idea of creative intelligences throughout the cosmos makes a lot more sense than a collection of abstract mathematical equations beyond space and time, with creativity itself just a matter of chance.

Angelic Intuition

This is why angels are called intellectual beings, beings who understand. For even in our case the things we grasp immediately we say we see intellectually, we give the name understanding to our latent habitual capacity to intuit first principles. ... If our human souls were endowed with an angelic abundance of intellectual light, then in the very act of intuiting first principles, we would understand all their consequences; we would know by intuition all that reasoning can deduce from them. ... [28] We humans have a dimness of intellectual light in our souls. But this light is at its full strength in an angel who, as Dionysius says, is a pure and brilliant mirror.[29]

Matthew: Aquinas is saying that angels are experts in intuition; they see things directly, with a pure understanding that he identifies with light. This may be one reason that angels are so closely connected with light; it's the light of knowledge and truth. We have the phrase "a light goes on"—we're in the dark and then a light goes on. Aquinas

---

28. ST 1, q. 58, a. 3.
29. ST 1, q. 58, a. 4.

is saying that for angels, in effect, the light is always on; they're always seeing the basic connections between things, effortlessly.

He stresses elsewhere that whereas human knowledge comes as much by discursive reasoning and struggle as by intuition, angels are paragons of intuition. They must be close friends of artists and all those who are in tune with their intuition, therefore.

Rupert: It's certainly true that when we talk about understanding, we can hardly avoid using the metaphor of light. And it's more than a metaphor: we see things with a kind of inner light. Our "mind's eye" works because our minds are somehow luminous.

The trouble is, not all our intuitions or creative jumps are correct. For example, a scientific hypothesis is a guess or an intuition about the way things are. But then we have to test by experiment to see if it's right or wrong. It's only too possible to have brilliant theories that turn out to be wrong. According to Aquinas's understanding of angels, if they have brilliant theories, they turn out to be right. They're not so much theories as direct insights into the way things are.

Divine Light

God is not unknown on account of obscurity but on account of the abundance of brightness. For the vision of God is by its essence above the nature of any creative intellect, not only human but even angelic.[30] God's radiance is super-substantial. That is, divine truth itself exceeds all boundaries and the ends of any knowledge.[31]

Matthew: Aquinas frequently emphasizes how angels differ from human beings and have a fuller abundance of intellectual light, but nevertheless he's at pains to demonstrate how angels are not

---

30. Cited in Fox, *Sheer Joy*, 201.
31. Cited in Fox, *Sheer Joy*, 2 1.

thoroughly godlike in their powers. They too have limits because they are creatures. For all their immense powers of intuition they do not see God face-to-face, so to speak—they do not experience the essence of the divine. It would be too much like our staring at the sun; it would render even their vision obscure and damage it.

Rupert: This passage reminds me of the Tibetan Book of the Dead, according to which, soon after you die you encounter a dazzling light. Only those who've prepared themselves through spiritual practice to face this light are able to go into it, and are thus liberated.

Most people can't bear it and turn aside. They are terrified. They are then shown a series of lesser lights, from which they also turn aside. They gradually come back to a plane of being where they start having sexual fantasies and become disembodied voyeurs around copulating couples until they're trapped in a womb and born again in a human body.

Matthew: As you say, the way to enter into this realm of beauty and light and the terror that accompanies it is spiritual practice. This is what the mystics mean by *via negativa*, the emptying process, the winnowing and pruning by which we learn to let go and surrender to the light, to a love force that's greater than us. Without this emptying process, this *kenosis*, we can survive only in a world such as we're in. In that sense we choose our future depending on how we have allowed ourselves to be pruned in this lifetime.

Again we're back to the dialectic of light and darkness. In the darkness we prepare ourselves for more light. There are many ways to resist the darkness, such as addictions, or denial, or just living a superficial life. If we refuse to go into that emptying process, that darkened area of the soul, then we're not going to have the capacity carved out in us to receive a fuller experience of light.

Death is both a dark experience and a light experience. It's darkness because it's unknown and involves fear and mystery. But those who have in some way acquired information about what happens after death come up with light imagery. It seems that death also contains immense light and may well be a return to the source of all light.

In the first creation story in Genesis, the first being made is light. Light is very close to the divine, the Godhead. It was on God's mind, the first thing made. And today's creation story begins with a fireball.

Rupert: In the earliest stages of Big Bang, in the primal fireball, light and darkness are not really differentiated; the primal fire transcended light and darkness as we know them. But as the universe expanded and cooled, there was then what's called the uncoupling of matter and radiation, the separation of matter from light. In other words, in the contemporary creation story, as in the book of Genesis, the differentiation of light from darkness is preceded by a state transcending both, a kind of fire that is beyond light or darkness.

The Nature of Understanding

The universe would be incomplete without intellectual creatures. And since understanding cannot be an act of the body or of bodily energies—body as such being limited to the here and now—it follows that a complete universe must contain some incorporeal creature. ... Hence, the incorporeal substances are midway between God and corporeal things and the point midway between extremes appears extreme with respect to either; the tepid compared with the hot seems cold. Hence the angels might be called material and bodily as compared with God, without implying that they are so intrinsically.[32]

Rupert: This discussion reminds me of David Bohm's idea of the implicate order. The phenomenal world, the world we live in, is the

---

32. ST 1, q. 50, a. 1.

explicate order, the unfolded order. Behind or beyond it is the implicate order, an enfolded order from which the world we experience arises. But Bohm doesn't just have one implicate order; he has a whole series of levels of orders that are more and more enfolded. There are levels of implicitness within the implicate order.

Looking outward, as it were, from within the implicate order toward the explicate, the next level looks like a body because it's on the bodily side of things. Looking inward, the more implicate level looks more like understanding, significance, or meaning. It is more like an idea. Bohm calls this double aspect of things "soma-significance."

Matthew: I find that idea of David Bohm's exciting because it puts our thought processes in a context beyond merely human epistemology. He's talking about the cosmic relationships that we undergo as thinkers, as beings that understand, as intellectual beings. As our understanding grows, there is a gradual unfolding from implicate to explicate. Maybe it is even our task to make more explicate what is implicate. In that sense we are contributing as a species to the self-awareness of the universe.

Intellects and Bodies

The activity of understanding is wholly non-material. ...[33] The act of understanding is not an action of the body or of any bodily energy. Hence to be joined to a body is not of the essence of intellectual being. ... Not all intellects are conjoined with bodies; there are some that exist separately, and these we call angels.[34]

Matthew: This means we human beings have company as a species with these other beings who, like us, seek understanding and have genuine intuitions about the truth of things. According to Aquinas, we're slowed down in the process by the fact that all our

33. ST 1, q. 50, a. 2.
34. ST 1, q. 5 1, a. 1.

knowledge comes by way of sense experience and discursive reasoning. But the experience of truth itself we have in common with angels.

We also have a responsibility to create, to give birth to a more explicit understanding of the world. This is a passion within us. That's why we enjoy truth. We sense that it's part of the creative process of the universe to discover some of its fundamental habits and its subtle interconnections.

Rupert: This drive for, as it were, disembodied knowledge has been extremely strong in the whole history of the development of science. Descartes talked about the scientific intellect as a kind of disembodied mind, rising beyond the immediate data of the senses and capable of understanding the ultimate laws of nature.

Matthew: Often I and others criticize Descartes for being the father of dualism in the West, splitting spirit and matter apart. And yet here in our conversation about angelic knowledge we're conceding that part of Descartes's world picture is something we need to pay attention to, namely, that our spirit nature is capable of going beyond the particular to the universal.

But we always have to get back to the particular because this is where morality happens or doesn't happen. Descartes, by so specializing on our angelic side, abstraction, really ignores the bodily side and therefore the heart and the lower chakras, including moral outrage. Descartes's philosophy is useful to us to the extent that we are angel-like, but it's very dangerous to build a civilization on a philosophy based on what we have in common with angelic, knowing beings. Now we're paying the price. Because of our flight from nature, from the Earth body and our own bodies, we have an ecological crisis, much of it stemming from ignorance of our relationship to the corporeal.

Rupert: Yes. Descartes was all in favor of angels. He thought he was inspired by one himself. He placed the human intellect, angels, and God in the spiritual realm, and in that respect he followed quite closely the medieval tradition. Whereas Aquinas recognized a threefold division of body, soul, and spirit, Descartes made a dualism by eliminating the middle term, the soul. This left just bodies, conceived of as inanimate machines, and spirit.

Matthew: In doing this he was following his mentor, St. Augustine, who defined spirit as "whatever is not matter."

Each Angel its Own Species

It is impossible that there should be more than one angel in a species. ... The value of a species outweighs the value of an individual as such. Hence a multiplication of angelic species is of far greater value than any number of individuals in one such species would be.[35]

Matthew: Aquinas, following Aristotle, regarded matter as the principle of individuation, or individuality. An eagle, for example, shares its general form and qualities with all other members of its species, but its material body gives it its individual existence, located in place and time. Since Aquinas taught that angels do not contain matter, there could only be a single angel in a species. Thus Aquinas celebrates every angel as a unique species, a species unique in itself.

Rupert: This means that each of the innumerable angels is different. Not different just as one blackbird differs from another blackbird, but different as a blackbird differs from a seagull.

Can Angels Assume Bodies?

Some have maintained that angels never assume bodies and that all the angelic appearances of which we read in the scriptures

---

35. ST 1, q. 50, a. 4.

were prophetic visions; that is, they took place in the imagination. But this goes against the sense of the scriptures; for what is seen only in someone's imagination is a purely private experience; it is not a thing that anyone else can see at the same time. But the scriptures speak of angels appearing visible to everyone who happened to be present in a given place; those seen by Abraham, for example, were also seen by his servants, and by Lot and by the people of Sodom; and the angel seen by Tobias was seen by everyone else who was present. Such visions must obviously have been corporeal, that is, of things existing outside the subject seeing. Since then angels are not themselves bodies, nor does their nature involve union with a body, we must conclude that they have sometimes assumed bodies. Hence angels do not need bodies for their own sake but for ours.[36]

Matthew: Aquinas insists that angels, as regards their own nature, are not corporeal. Nevertheless, he feels strongly that angels do assume bodies or what appear to be bodies in their work, in governing the universe, and especially in relating to people.

Rupert: I think it's interesting that Aquinas in this passage deals with what we think of as a modern view: if people say they see angels, these are just things in their own minds or their own imaginations; angels do not really exist out there.

Matthew: Yes. He's insisting that angelic experiences are not purely private, that our imaginations are not strictly subjective. He is saying that angelic encounters are experiences of truth that can be intersubjective. They appeal to the imagination of many people, and this cuts through the dualism of subject versus object.

When he says, "Such visions must obviously have been corporeal, that is, of things existing outside the subject seeing," I

---

36. ST 1, q. 51, a. 2.

think that's an interesting definition of corporeal: corporeal things exist outside the subject seeing. Modern philosophy seems unable to get out of the head and recognize that things exist whether we know them or not.

I like his very direct statement, "Angels do not need bodies for their own sake but for ours." It's the power of angelic generosity to take on bodily form to assist us, to help us, to communicate with us, and to be recognized by us. He seems to be saying that anyone who is going to help us in some way has to become incarnated.

In fact, immediately after this passage, Aquinas goes on to allude to Christ assuming a human body. Incarnation seems to be a necessary means by which human beings learn anything, including even the divine.

Rupert: This assumption of bodies is important in two contexts. One is the appearances of guardian angels. Many recent books about encounters with guardian angels involve angels appearing in human form to help people out. The other is the portrayal of angels. If angels don't have bodily forms, you can't have pictures of them. And there are innumerable pictures of angels.

Angels are, of course, often portrayed as having wings. According to Aquinas, angels don't by their very nature need bodies, let alone wings. Nor do they need wings to move around. He's saying that they only take on a bodily appearance for our sake, and presumably they're conventionally pictured with wings to represent their ability to move quickly from place to place.

Matthew: I don't recall any place in all of Aquinas's writings about angels where he ever once mentions wings. But the image of wings has an archetypal power, and suggests not just movement but soaring. That is integral to mystical experience. Wings also bring to mind the eagle and other great birds as spirit beings. They get a perspective on things by being high, and also have the freedom up there to soar. That is something we yearn for. It's part of our mystical nature, to soar. Artists have projected that onto their images of angels.

Revelation and Prophecy: The Work of the Angels

The spirit works grace in people by means of the angels.[37] The divine enlightenments and revelations are conveyed from God to humans by the angels. Now, prophetic knowledge is bestowed by divine enlightenment and revelation. Therefore it is evident it is conveyed by the angels.[38] Prophecy is a perfection of the intellect, in which an angel also can form an impression.[39] Prophetic revelation which is conveyed by the ministry of the angels is said to be divine revelation.[40] Prophecy is between the angels and the people.[41]

Matthew: This is a very important understanding in Aquinas about angels. The image I have when he talks about angels carrying divine enlightenments and revelations is that of bees carrying pollen from flower to flower. This idea is that angels carry prophetic revelations from prophet to prophet. In other words, new ideas. This really fits with his understanding of angelic knowledge; the angels are experts at intuition. And so are prophets. They have moral intuition.

I hear him saying that angels carry messages and seeds of intuition from person to person. Maybe this is one reason that, in a time like ours when a prophetic consciousness is so needed, there's a consensus growing among different kinds of people, from scientists to theologians to poets to environmentalists and so forth. When we talk about a consensus rising or a worldview arising, perhaps angels really

---

37. ST 11, q. 172; cited in Fox, *Sheer Joy*, 470-471.
38. ST, a. 2.
39. ST, ad. 1.
40. ST, ad. 3.
41. Cited in Fox, *Sheer Joy*, 466.

have a role in this. After all, where do our dreams come from and where do our intuitions come from?

"Prophetic revelation" is a very strong term. "Divine enlightenment" and prophetic revelation. That these are conveyed by the ministry of angels really gives them a tremendous task to do in a time of social, intellectual, and ecological discontinuity. Such is the time we're living in. The rebirth of civilization and the hope for a renaissance rely as much on angels as on human goodwill and commitment.

Rabbi Heschel says the prophet interferes, but Aquinas is saying the interference is not just emotional or rhetorical, but intellectual. Just as the struggle for justice is an intellectual thing. You can't have a struggle for justice without an intellectual life because it's about weighing possibilities—an image we have in the archetype of the blind woman with the scales.

Rupert: I think Aquinas's ideas about revelation and enlightenment through the angels are also important in restoring to us a sense of inspiration. All great art and, indeed, all great creativity are based on the idea of inspiration, breathed in from a conscious being or intelligence higher than ourselves. And this is conveyed in the classical concept of the genius, the spirit that leads or guides a person.

The classical poets began with an invocation to their muse, asking her to guide and inspire them. This tradition continued in English poetry, as in Spenser's *Faerie Queene* and Milton's *Paradise Lost*. And today if you go to a concert of classical music in South India, it starts with an invocation to Sarasvati, the goddess of wisdom and music.

The idea of information coming from higher sources has recently undergone a popular revival and is only too common nowadays. We have a cacophony of channeling going on. In any New Age bookshop, there's volume after volume of channeled information. Although I love the idea of angelic inspiration, I must admit to a prejudice against all this channeling.

Matthew: This is where Aquinas's treatment in this passage is so refreshing. He insists on the intellectual dimension. And the prophetic dimension is a justice dimension. These are the two dimensions that I think are often lacking in New Age channeling. For example, a lot of these channelers are busy making money on their angels, and where does it go? Who is it serving? And what is the intellectual content of this?

There is such a thing as right-brain excess. An approach to angels that does not include a tradition such as Aquinas represents, with its dimensions of intellectual life and prophetic life, makes for a slippery relationship with the angelic world. The real interest of the angels is to help humankind and to serve. But channeling can end up simply serving people's monetary or ego or fame needs. I too am very ill at ease with treatments of angels that do not demonstrate that the result is one of compassion for the human situation and for the earth situation. This is why Aquinas being so explicit about the prophetic role of the angels is such refreshing news.

Divine Silence

Angels are announcers of divine silence. For it is clear that a conception of the heart or of the intellect that is without voice is with silence. But it is through a perceptible voice that silence of the heart is proclaimed. ... Angels are always announcers of divine silence. But it is necessary after something is announced to someone that they understand the announcement. In addition, therefore, because we can understand by the intellect the things that are announced to us through the angels, they themselves by the brightness of their own light help our intellect grasp the secrets of God.[42]

---

42. Cited in Fox, *Sheer Joy*, 216-217.

Matthew: I think that's a very beautiful task that Aquinas names the angels as performing: to be announcers of divine silence. And angels not only do the announcing but help us in understanding announcements. They touch our intellects by the brightness of their own light.

I think that we have lost respect for silence. Our worlds are filled with Muzak and television and all these intrusions on nature's silence. Silence is becoming rarer and rarer. Yet spiritual traditions have always taught that silence is one of the ways in which the heart is open and the divine speaks to us. A Quaker meeting is one example, and many kinds of meditation, from Zen Buddhism to monastic meditation, involve sitting in silence.

I think this news that angels bring silence is part of our recovering a sacred cosmology. I remember Rusty Schweickart, the astronaut, talking about how it was the cosmic silence out in space that made him a mystic, after having trained for years as a jet-fighter pilot. People who go to the depths of the sea or scuba dive have talked to me about the awesome silence down there. Silence is clearly one of the ways into the heart, into the divine mystery. It's a very special task and a very mysterious one that Aquinas names here in this simple sentence, "Angels are announcers of divine silence."

Rupert: Does this mean that one way that we contact the angels is through being silent? It would suggest that whenever we go into a silent space through meditation, insofar as that silence is divine, then the announcement of the divine presence is made through an angel.

Matthew: That's right, angels are present. Silence is like a vacuum that sucks angels in. They can't resist sacred silence. But we don't always approach silence through meditation, though that's the obvious route. My experience is that whenever there's an experience of awe, there's an experience of silence as well. In doing ritual, for example, which may not be a silent ritual, when you are doing good prayer, it always raises silence. If that's true, then it's also true that good prayer raises the angels; it makes present the angels.

Rupert: But it's a very paradoxical statement about angels as announcers of divine silence, because to announce usually involves sound.

Matthew: Yes. Now and again Aquinas has these kinds of statements that really awaken us. I think he's deliberately being paradoxical, to announce divine silence.

Rupert: "For it is clear that a conception of the heart or of the intellect that is without voice is with silence."

Matthew: I think that is referring to the nature of the angels, that they do not have voice. This makes angels especially adept at silence. Remember, they learn through intuition and when you think about it, isn't intuition in some ways a nonverbal thing? In that sense, it's a more direct link to both the heart and the mind.

Rupert: Would that mean then that the kind of communication they have with us is more like telepathy than regular hearing?

Matthew: Yes, I think he is implying that. Or that they even ride in on our intuitions and our dreams. When you're dreaming, you're silent, and I think angels are attracted and allured by that.

Rupert: "But it is through a perceptible voice that silence of the heart is proclaimed." Is he saying that to proclaim what we find in the silence of the heart, we have to use our voices?

Matthew: Yes, we proclaim and we praise. And that's essentially what we have voices for, to proclaim the mystery and what we've learnt in the silence of our hearts.

Rupert: I still don't see how this fits with the traditional view of the choirs of angels singing, "Holy, holy, holy."

Matthew: That's a good point. But it's both/and. What makes artists speak out is the depth of silence they've experienced before. In other words, they have something to say that reaches the depth of mystery. They're not just making noise; it's coming out of a true silence. All prayer has to come out of a deep silence of some kind, and that includes angelic prayer.

It's in the silence that we gather our truth and the emptying takes place. It's the *via negativa* that precedes the *via creativa*. That emptying allows the spirits to enter. And another word for the spirits is angels.

Poet M. C. Richards asks, "In the beginning was the word, but what preceded the word?" Her answer is: silence. The authentic word comes out of silence.

Working with Angels

We do the works that are of God along with the holy angels.[43]

Matthew: To me this is a statement of our being co-workers with God, and how being a co-worker with God also means we are co-workers with the angels. To do our godly work we have invisible helpers, the angels. This is good news. I think we need all the help we can get for the spiritual work we need to do today There are experiences one has in dreams and intuitions and insights, and even in defense and healing, that are more readily explained by angelic presence than by any other cause.

Rupert: But for the last two or three hundred years many people, including Christians, have not taken angels very seriously. They've been regarded as relics of a bygone age, as mythical beings with wings. Yet if angels are real, in whatever sense they're real, they've been there all along and they've been helping people all along. Or in the case of bad angels, hindering them.

How much do you think that working with the angels requires a conscious acknowledgment of them, or even an invocation of the

---

43. Cited in Fox, *Sheer Joy*, 16 1.

angels? If they've been helping all along, even though people haven't been aware of them, then it means they can work with a very low profile and also in a way that doesn't seem to require people to say "please" and "thank you." They just do it anyway.

But how much more might they help if we do acknowledge their presence? And how should we acknowledge their presence and call on their help?

Matthew: That's a very good question, and a practical one. One point that Aquinas keeps coming back to is that, after all, we are conscious beings ourselves. Angels do not interfere with our choices or with our mysteries, the secrets of our hearts. Therefore, it would seem to me that it's very important that we call on them. Otherwise, their work is relegated to external affairs. The real work we have to do is in terms of imagination, creativity, intuition, birthing new forms of everything from politics to education. If we want angelic help, we're going to have to invite them into our personal minds and hearts, and also our collective minds and hearts.

It is possible that during the modern era, when we banished angels effectively from our minds, hearts, thoughts, and institutions, they more or less left. Maybe they're busy on another planet where they are more welcome. Part of the wonder of reinvigorating worship will be an awareness that angels are present again. They have to be invoked. And the point you made is very important—that they be thanked.

Rupert: This would give a more than usual significance to the feast of St. Michael and All Angels on 29 September, the day in the liturgical calendar when they are most fully acknowledged, even though many of those who acknowledge them are puzzled as to what they are doing. But this still exists as an important part of the church calendar. One way to acknowledge them is to make more conscious this traditional festival.

In the Jewish tradition there are rituals and prayers for the angels. Maybe there are a lot in the Christian tradition. Do you think that if we studied more closely the texts of the Middle Ages, when angels were taken more seriously and frequently portrayed in churches and cathedrals, we would find prayers and practices relating to the angels that could serve as a starting point for us today?

Matthew: Absolutely. In Western liturgy, the preface of the mass includes several explicit prayers in which the angels are invoked. The song "Holy, holy, holy" is a song of the angels, sung in the prophetic books of the Hebrew Bible. So the angels are really present in every eucharistic mass, provided we pray in a cosmological setting. But as you say, we've been numbed to this, and during the last few centuries perhaps it hasn't meant that much. In fact, perhaps we've been embarrassed by it.

In the Middle Ages a tremendous amount of speculation and experience with angels was being articulated. Clearly, the consciousness of the people was that there are spirits that have to be dealt with, both allies and tricksters and foes. This is not just a Christian reality; it's a reality of the native people in America certainly and, as far as we can tell, among all peoples. It's part of a deep ecumenism of our time. Returning to an awareness of praying with the angels, and having the good angels assist us and standing up to the bad angels, this is part of the pilgrimage we're making together as a species into our deepest spiritual wells and traditions. Deep ecumenism requires an awakening to the powers of the spirits and angels. And the angels will awaken us.

How Are Angels Localized?

An angel is in a place by a power contact. If you like to call this contact an action (*operatio*) because action is the proper effect of power, you can say, an angel is in a place by acting there—provided that "action" be understood in a sense that includes not only active movement (*motio*), but also any kind of conjunction (*unitio*) whereby an angel brings its power into connection with the body, whether governing it or containing it or in any other way.[44] It does not follow that an angel is ever contained by a place; for the application to a body of a power of a spiritual substance is, in effect, a containing of the body by that substance and not vice versa. Thus the human soul itself is in the body as containing it and not as contained by it. In somewhat the same way, an angel is in a given bodily place not as contained by, but as containing it.[45]

Matthew: Obviously it's difficult to talk about angels in place since angels, by definition, have no body. Place seems to be a quality of a bodily thing. I'm struck by the way Aquinas names the presence of angels as being directly linked to their action. An angel is in a place by acting there. These actions include not only movement but also union or connection, perhaps relationship.

The point that angels are not contained by a place but are actually containing the place is a bit mysterious. It makes the angels' presence different from what we're used to on a regular basis.

Rupert: It seems to me that fields once again provide the closest analogy. For example, we wouldn't say that the universal gravitational field is contained by the universe; we'd say that the universe is contained by the field. Likewise, the electromagnetic field, through which light travels, contains what it's acting on. The electromagnetic field around us now, through which we can see things, and be seen, contains us. It acts on us and we act on it.

This brings us again to the question of angels and photons. A photon is a quantum of action. Photons are localized through their action, just as Aquinas says angels are. There is a further similarity in that a photon is not material in the normal sense of the word. The photon has no mass. In other words, it's not really a body; it's incorporeal.

---

44. *Quaestiones Quodlibetales* (Quod.). 1, 4.
45. ST 1, q. 52, a. 2.

So I think that science provides us with important metaphors or parallels to the idea of angels as immaterial and disembodied but capable of containing bodies and being present through their action. In fact, that's what quantum theory's all about.

Matthew: Can you call a field a place?

Rupert: You can't call a field a place. You can say that a field has a place in which it acts. And fields have a certain localization; but if you talk about a field that contains an electron, for example, there's a sense in which the electron field is spread out with a decreasing probability over an infinite distance. Fields don't have rigid boundaries. A magnetic field around a magnet does not have sharp edges: it spreads out with diminishing power indefinitely. The gravitational field of the earth keeps the moon in its orbit and influences the sun and planets. It also has an influence on distant stars and galaxies, but so small as to be negligible.

Matthew: I think it's amazing that these analogies exist between Aquinas's thinking and imagination and today's scientific thinking and imagination. It's fascinating that Aquinas's mind, when thinking about angels, got into the kinds of relationship that today's science is also playing with. Angels and photons, there we have it.

Angels Act in One Place at a Time

When we relate anything to a single power, to that extent we unify it. Thus as related to the universal power of God, the whole universe is one thing; and similarly any part of the universe, as related to the power of an angel, is one thing. Since then an angel is in place inasmuch as his power is applied to a place, he is never simply everywhere at once, nor in several places, but in one place only at a given moment. ... It is not necessary that the place where an angel is should be spatially indivisible; it can be divisible or indivisible, greater or less, according as the angel chooses, voluntarily, to apply his power to a more or less extended body. And the whole body, whatever it be, will be as one place to him.[46]

Rupert: Here the analogy with fields comes out even more clearly. A field is a whole. You can't have a bit of a magnetic field, for example. If you chop up a magnet into little bits, each part of the magnet is a complete magnet with a complete magnetic field. If you put the little bits of magnet together to form one magnet, all the fields join up to form a single magnetic field.

It's the nature of fields that they unify the things on which they're acting, relating them together as a whole. For example, the gravitational field of the solar system relates the sun and planets together, giving the system its unity.

In biology, the morphogenetic fields that shape the body have the same quality. The morphogenetic field that shapes a giraffe embryo as it grows brings together under its influence all the developing organs; it coordinates their growth so that they develop and work together to make up a giraffe. The field relates the parts together as a unity, as a living organism.

Aquinas's views fit well with modern field theories, but they go further. Field theories resemble the medieval conception of the soul as that which organized and contained a living body. Aquinas himself makes this point and draws a parallel between the containing nature of the soul and the way in which angels are present in places. But the action of angels goes beyond that of souls or fields; it is not an unconscious and habitual part of the course of nature—it involves consciousness and choice.

Matthew: That is something Aquinas underscores when he says the angel chooses voluntarily to apply its power to a more or less

---

46. ST 1, q. 52, a. 2.

extended body. There's a choice on the part of the angel, a willingness and an option to be creative in this or that place, connected to these or those bodies. A love option, therefore.

Angelic Love

The will of angels is by nature loving.[47] Angels cannot help loving, by force of nature.[48]

Matthew: I think it's important that we're not just dealing with knowing beings but loving beings. Angelic powers are not neutral. Einstein said that the most important question you can ask in life is this: "Is the universe friendly or not?" Aquinas is saying that these angelic beings that are governing the universe are loving beings.

We don't tend to look on fields as necessarily loving. They play out their role in the universe, which is sustaining and making things possible. But here we have beings that are also nurturing, caring, and loving. Here we have a confirmation that the interconnectivity in the universe is not just impersonal, but depends on compassionate beings that love and care.

Rupert: I think that's an important addition. The gravitational field unifies the whole universe. Like love, it is unifying by its nature. But we usually think of gravitational attraction as a completely unconscious process. To introduce this element of consciousness goes far beyond the field concept of contemporary science.

Matthew: And we have metaphors connecting gravity and love, for example, "falling in love." If we deanthropocentrize our language, including the phrase "falling in love," we might realize how much we are loved by cosmic forces like angels. And this might sustain us at times when human love fails us.

---

47. ST 1, q. 60, a. 2.
48. ST 1, q. 60, a. 5

Can Several Angels Be in the Same Place at Once?

No two souls exist in the same body and similarly no two angels exist in the same place. Two angels cannot be in the same place at once because it is impossible that one and the same thing should depend entirely and immediately on two causes. ... In so far as its power is applied to a given place, and so is containing it completely, we can conclude that only one angel can be in that place at a given time.[49]

Matthew: This question is as close as Aquinas gets to the oft-repeated caricature of scholastic angelotogy, where we've been told they spent years arguing over how many angels could dance on the head of a pin.

Rupert: How did this caricature come into being?

Matthew: I have never in my rather extensive reading of medieval literature and theology ever seen the question raised, much less dwelled on. I think the rationalist historians and philosophers of the last few centuries found it necessary to put down the Middle Ages. In fact, a lot of people have been raised to believe the Middle Ages were the dark ages entirely. But this is hard to believe if you visit Chartres Cathedral or the many other great cathedrals from that age. Obviously they knew a lot about engineering, to say nothing of stained glass and cosmology and how to connect religion to cosmos and spirit.

Rupert: What Aquinas is saying in this passage is that just as you couldn't have two souls containing the same body, so you can't have two angels working on the same system. The nature of the soul is that it's the unifying principle of the body, so to have two souls working on the same body would deny this unifying quality unless they alternated.

Matthew: Like Dr. Jekyll and Mr. Hyde?

---

49. ST 1, q. 52, a. 3

Rupert: Yes. Even in the most extreme multiple-personality cases, with dozens of personalities, they follow one another successively rather than acting at the same time. Likewise, in a TV set you can see different channels one after another, but you can't see them all at the same time.

That analogy supports Aquinas's contention that there can't be two angels acting in the same place at the same time. But on the other hand, if we take the field metaphor for angels, there can be two fields operating at the same time. For example, the electromagnetic field is acting on my body; I can be seen and I can see. At the same time, the gravitational field that is acting on and through my body is holding me down on my seat so that I don't float off in the air. When a guardian angel is acting on a person, the person is also on earth, and the angel of the earth contains and can act upon the whole environment within which that person and his or her guardian angel are acting. So Aquinas's system would allow for two angels working in the same place at the same time if they're angels of different size and scope.

How Angels Move

An angel is in contact with a given place simply and solely through his power there. Hence his movement from place to place can be nothing but a succession of distinct power contacts; and I say succession, because, as we have seen, an angel is not in more than one place at a time. And such contacts need not be continuous. … The angelic movement too may be continuous. But it may, on the other hand, take place as an instantaneous transference of power from the whole of one place to the whole of another; and in this case the angel's movement will be discontinuous.[50] We have already seen that the local movement of an angel can

---

50. ST 1, q. 53, a. 1

be continuous or discontinuous. When continuous it necessarily entails a passing through an intermediate place.[51] If an angel's movement is discontinuous, it does not cross all the intermediate places between its starting place and its term. This kind of movement—from one extreme of a given space to another, immediately—is possible for an angel, but not for a body; for a body is measured and contained by place and so must obey the laws of place in its movements. Not so an angel: far from being subject to and contained by place, its substance dominates and contains it. An angel can apply itself to a given place as it pleases, either passing through other places, or not.[52]

Rupert: I suppose one way in which an angel could move continuously is by acting on something that's moving. For example, if a person on whom a guardian angel is acting moves around, the angel's movement will be continuous, just as the movement of the person is continuous; as it goes from one place to another, it goes through the places in between.

More interesting is the idea of discontinuous movement, in which an angel, as it were, jumps from one place in which it was acting to another without needing to pass through all the places in between.

In quantum theory, in between one action and another, an entity such as a photon or electron exists as a "wave function." And this wave function is spread out in space as a probability distribution. You can't say exactly where it is. It's only when it acts that it's localized. The whole spread-out wave of probability collapses to a particular point. This is called the "collapse of the wave function."

One of the paradoxes of quantum theory is if you have single photons going one at a time through an apparatus with two slits, even

---

51. ST 1, q. 53, a. 2
52. ST 1, q. 53, a. 2

though there's only one going through at a time, you get interference patterns on a photographic film as if the photons have been traveling as waves through both slits. These waves then collapse as a photon acts on a particular silver grain in the photographic film.

Interestingly, in quantum theory the wave function is represented mathematically by a many-dimensional formula; it's not in ordinary three-dimensional space. When it's in between locations where it acts, it's in a kind of imaginary space that exists as a mathematical reality but not as a physical reality.

Quantum entities such as photons are discontinuous in their action. When a photon leaves the sun, there's a quantum of action there. When it hits something on Earth and illuminates it, there's another action. But in between, the photon can only be represented by a wave function spread out through space. As soon as it acts, you can locate it. But that doesn't tell you that it was previously localized in that place, only that through its action it collapses or condenses in that place. Its tendency to act in one place or another can be predicted only in terms of probability. It has a measure of indeterminism or freedom.

So the issues Aquinas deals with here in relation to the movement of angels are similar to the ideas about the movement of photons and other quantum particles in quantum theory.

Matthew: Does this amaze you as much as it amazes me? I mean, I'm coming at it from the point of view of the history of theology, and I think it's just stunning to find Aquinas's mind in the thirteenth century playing with the same questions that quantum physics is playing with today: continuity, discontinuity, action in place, and what's going on in between. Are you surprised to find this in a medieval thinker?

Rupert: Yes, I was astonished to find it. Part of my interest in Aquinas's work on angels was awakened precisely by seeing these parallels. I think the parallels arise because he's dealing with the same question: How can something nonmaterial and indivisible move and act on bodies located in particular places?

Matthew: You can only come up with so many answers to that question. It's interesting that the action of photons and the action of angels both involve an element of freedom, but in the case of angels Aquinas emphasizes the importance of conscious choice: "An angel can apply itself to a given place as it pleases."

Is An Angel's Movement Instantaneous?

An angel can move in discontinuous time. He can be now here and now there with no time-interval between.[53] When an angel moves the beginning and the end of his movement do not take place in two instants between which there is any time; nor again does the beginning occupy a stretch of time which an instant at the end terminates; but the beginning is in one instant and the end in another. Between these there is no time at all. Let us say then that an angel's movement is in time, but not in the way that bodily movements are.[54]

Matthew: If I'm not mistaken, Rupert, this is what first got you excited about angels and photons, the idea that time does not elapse when angels relocate. Doesn't that come very close to what we think about photons too?

Rupert: Yes. A photon can be in one place at one instant, say when light leaves the sun; then it can be at another place at another instant, as when the light from the sun hits something on the earth and lights it up. It's about eight minutes in the normal measure of time between those instants. So we can assign a speed to light.

53. ST 1, q. 53, a. 3
54. Quod. XI, 4.

But according to relativity theory—and this was one of the starting points for Einstein—from the point of view of the photon itself, no time elapses. There is an instantaneous connection between the light leaving the sun and hitting something on Earth, and the photon is not aging.

The so-called cosmic microwave background radiation is believed to be light left over from the Big Bang, and indeed is one of the main lines of evidence for the occurrence of the Big Bang some 14 billion years ago. Those photons are as old as anything can possibly be, but they haven't worn out, because in themselves they're timeless. We could use Aquinas's words to describe the movement of a photon: "The beginning is in one instant and the end in another. Between these there is no time at all. Let us say then that [a photon's] movement is in time, but not in the way that bodily movements are."

An important feature of relativity theory is that no body can move at the speed of light, because as bodies start moving close to the speed of light, their mass goes up. At the speed of light itself, their mass would be infinite. So only light can move at the speed of light, and it can do so because photons are massless.

Matthew: This notion that photons don't age is very interesting. Aquinas said angels don't age. This may provide some limited justification for the picturing, especially popular in the Baroque period, of angels as babies. You don't have the problem of the negative *senex* or the exhausted angel; that's a human problem, because we're connected to mass and to body.

Another way to put it is that the angels are in the eternal now. If no passage of time takes place in them when they move, they're not beset by the onslaught of past and future; they always exist in the now This makes them preeminent mystics, because the mystic in us also lives in the now.

Rupert: And photons exist in an eternal now. It is interesting that angels are often described as beings of light; the connection between light and angels has been made from the earliest times. It is not just a coincidence that we find remarkable parallels today between angels and the nature of light.

Matthew: We talk about a photon as both a particle and a wave. Maybe there's a hint here as regards angels, that at times their operation is more like a wave and at times their presence is more like a particle.

Rupert: The wave aspect of the photon has to do with nonlocalized nature and its movement. The particle aspect has to do with its localized action. Insofar as angels act in particular places, they are like particles; insofar as they are disembodied and mobile, they are like waves, vibrations in fields.

Imagination

Intellect in us is agent and potential, because of its relation to the imagination or to the phantasms. Forms in the imagination are related to the potential intellect as colors to the sense of sight but to the agent as colors to light. Now there is no imagination in angels; hence no reason to divide their intellects in this way.[55]

Matthew: Aquinas here takes up the subject of human imagination. He uses the medieval distinction between the potential intellect and the agent or active intellect. The potential intellect involves an awareness of ideas and concepts; the active intellect renders intelligible sensory impressions we receive from the material world. Together they signify what we mean by creativity or imagination.

He asks whether angels also have imagination and concludes that they do not. Our imagination links us to sensory knowledge, and

---

55. ST 1, q. 54, a. 4

angels do not have sensory knowledge. For Aquinas, imagination is half-way between sensory knowledge and spiritual knowledge. Those who are endowed with rich imagination—we would call them creative types or artists—are a link between the spiritual and the everyday for the rest of us.

Aquinas thought that the specifically human mode of understanding included the potential intellect and the agent intellect, a combination that connected intelligence to animality. And of course it's true. Animals dream. My dog would wake up with a nightmare now and again. Animals have a kind of imagination too, at least a playing over of their experiences and of their possible experiences.

One reason Aquinas denies that angels have imagination is because they live so fully in the now. Imagination is very connected to memory, to the past, and to the future. That's its power but also its weakness. People can live only in imagination in a culture like ours, even in other people's imaginations, such as advertisers'. Imagination can be a distraction from living in the now—but it does not have to be.

The gift of healthy art is that it takes the power of the imagination and brings us back to the now, to the depth and truth of what really is.

When Aquinas says that angels have no imagination, he actually honors this unique gift we have as human beings. While being spiritual like the angels, we're also sensate like the animals, and imagination is a bridge that can serve us; we can fill it with spiritual values and intelligence and energy. Or we can allow it to carry us simply into our base natures and not be moved beyond that.

Imagination sets us off from the angels. It shows how we have something they don't have. Another way to put it is, *Are angels artists?* Maybe that's one reason that traditionally they come to worship. Maybe they come to hear Mozart because they don't have any Mozarts. Maybe they come to Chartres Cathedral because no angel has constructed a cathedral. That's the human task. Worship and ritual are gifts of human imagination to raise the community energy to a level where the angels are as interested as we are. This is a kind of gift we make to the angels, the gift of our art, the gift of our imaginations.

Do Angels Know Particular Things?

Angels guard us individually, according to the words of the psalm, "He has given his angels charge over thee." ... If angels had no knowledge of individual things they could exercise no providential government over events in this world, since these always imply individuals at work. ... Administration and government and the causing of movement have to do with particulars existing in the here and now. ... As a man knows all classes of things by faculties that differ from each other—knowing by his intellect, universals, and things free from matter, and by sensation the particular and the corporeal—so an angel knows both kinds of beings by one and the same intellectual power. For such is the order of the universe, that the nobler a being is, the more unified and at the same time, the more wide-ranging is its power. ... Since then the angelic nature is superior to ours, it is unreasonable to deny that what man can know by one of his various faculties, an angel can know by a single and intellectual cognitive faculty.[56]

Matthew: This passage seems relevant to our discussions about the role of angels in an evolutionary universe. It would seem that Aquinas is saying that if we can know the historical unfolding of events, with an evolutionary sense of time, then certainly angels can know it too, though in a different way. First of all, they would know it intuitively, because that's the way they know everything. They would know it because it is part of reality, and somehow they

---

56. ST 1, q. 57, a. 2

know all of reality, though not through sense-knowledge but through another mode.

While our species only recently came up with the theory of the evolutionary nature of the universe, presumably angels knew things that medieval schoolmen and the church fathers never knew about the size of the universe, the age of the universe, and the evolutionary, creative nature of the universe. You might say that angels must have been frustrated all these centuries, waiting for human beings to catch up with some awareness of how magnificently creative the universe is, and how it has been so from the word go.

Rupert: I agree. I think this discussion of Aquinas is very important. In order to be administering spirits and guardian angels, they need to know what's actually going on in the world. And they don't have this by some kind of foreknowledge since, at least in the case of guardian angels, they are dealing with beings with free will.

Here Aquinas is seriously considering the ways angels interact with what's going on and know what's actually happening. He has to think of a way they know it directly, without the need for sense-knowledge, since they don't have senses.

If I had to try and conceive how angels could have a direct way of knowing without the mediation of bodily senses, I would start from the possibility that they somehow interact with the organizing fields of things. The mental activity of a person, the development of a plant, the formation of a snowflake, the whole activity of Gaia—all are organized by fields. So are atoms and galaxies. Perhaps the angel could interact directly with these fields. If the fields could act on the angel, and the angel directly experience their nature and present state, it would have a direct knowledge of what was going on within and around the organism with which it was interacting.

Aquinas thinks that this could happen through a "single and intellectual cognitive faculty." He also speaks of the way that the nobler a being is, the more unified and at the same time the more wide-ranging its power. An angel concerned with our entire planet would have a Gaian sphere of action and a unified knowledge of what's going on in the earth. One concerned with the Galaxy would have a knowledge of the entire galactic field and all the activities within it. The guardian angel of a person would have a unified and wide-ranging knowledge of that person's being through a direct cognition of the fields underlying the person's thoughts, actions, intentions, and relationships.

Angels do not merely know; they act. The fields of an organism act upon its guiding angel, and this action is the basis for the angel's direct knowledge of the organism's innermost being and becoming. Conversely, the angel can act upon the organism through its organizing fields, perturbing and giving new patterns to their activity.

In this way we can think of fields as the interface though which organisms and their guiding angels interact. Some such interaction is essential if angelic intelligences are to play guiding and creative roles in the evolutionary process.

Matthew: As you point out, when it comes to guardian angels, angels are working with people with free will. In another place Aquinas says that angels do not know the secrets in the hearts of human beings—only God does.[57] So not only do they not interfere with our choices, they couldn't even if they wanted to, because that's a sphere of knowledge that only God has access to.

I think that's important. The spirits are not dictating to us; they do not render us mere creatures of fate. They have to keep their distance from our own conscience and our own creativity, for example. They can assist, but they're in no way depriving us of our own power of choice.

But also what comes to my mind is the question of chance, especially in light of the evolutionary view. Granted that angels do not have control of beings with free will, we can also ask: What do angels

---

57. ST 1, q. 57, a. 4

know about the chance occurrences in the universe, the seemingly random occurrences that in fact end up in a new kind of order?

Do Angels Know The Future?

The future can be known in two ways. First, in its causes; and so future things which come necessarily from their causes can be known with certainty, as that the sun will rise tomorrow. Other things that come from their causes in most cases, are not foreknowable with certainty but with a measure of probability, as when a doctor forms an opinion on the future health of a patient. And this kind of foreknowledge is found in the angels, and at a higher degree than in man because they know the causes of things more extensively and more thoroughly than we do; as a doctor can pronounce more surely on the future course of an ailment the more clearly he sees into its causes. As for events which come from their causes on only relatively few occasions—casual and chance events—these cannot be known beforehand at all. ... By no created mind can the future be known as it is in itself. ... The angelic mind has its own sort of time arising from the succession of conceptions occurring in intelligence; so that Augustine can say, "God moves the spiritual creature through time." And because of this succession in the angelic mind, not all that happens through the whole course of time can be simultaneously present to it. ... Things existing in the present have a nature by which they resemble the ideas in an angel's mind, so that through these ideas they can be known to him. But what is yet to be has not yet got a nature through which to resemble those ideas; hence it cannot be known through them.[58]

---

58. ST 1, q. 57, a. 3

Matthew: This puts limits on angels' knowledge of evolutionary processes. It makes their knowledge and their power quite relative.

Rupert: Also the idea that there's time in angelic minds helps us to see how angels can be involved in evolution. If they had timeless, Platonic minds, there's no way they could be involved in an evolving cosmos. But if they know what's happening in the world by interacting with the things under their sphere of influence, and they have a succession of understandings, this is a basis for development or evolution in angelic minds. And through their evolving consciousness they play a creative part in the evolutionary process.

Matthew: That's an exciting idea. Even angels evolve. Although they are spiritual beings, their minds are evolving. Aquinas says: "What is yet to be has not yet got a nature through which to resemble those ideas; hence it cannot be known through them." In effect, he's saying angels learn.

Were The Angels Created Before The Physical Universe?

Were the angels created before the physical universe? On this point the writings of the Church Fathers show two opinions. But the more probable one is that the angels and corporeal creatures were created simultaneously. ... It seems unlikely that God, whose "works are perfect," as we read in Deuteronomy, should have created the angels on their own before the rest of creation. However, the contrary view should not be called an error. ... The Greek Fathers all held that the angels were created before the corporeal universe. ... If the angels were made before the universe of bodies then in the text of Genesis, "In the beginning God created heaven and Earth," the words, "In the beginning" must be interpreted as "In the Son" or "In the beginning of time"; but not as "In the beginning before which nothing existed," unless this be referred exclusively to corporeal things.[59]

Rupert: It seems that Aquinas thought that the angels were created along with the physical universe because all creation hung together and was interrelated (see the text on page 76). The angels have a role to play in relation to corporeal things, not on their own; hence they were not a separate creation prior to the physical universe. That makes sense to me. The intelligences or ministering spirits that organize corporeal things come into being with them. In an evolutionary universe, that would mean that as new things come into being, the angels that guide them come into being together with them: new angels would arise as galaxies appear, and as new stars, planets, species of plants and animals, and human societies come into being.

We now have a much more extended view of creation than Aquinas did, or indeed anyone else did until the cosmological revolution of the 1960s. This would give us a much more extended view of the creation of angels. New angels would be created as the things to which they're related are created, in a process extending over some 14 billion years of cosmic evolution and continuing today.

The view of the Greek fathers is like the conventional view in science; that is, both views are Platonic. The laws of nature are regarded as eternal mathematical truths existing beyond space and time. They were already there at the moment of the Big Bang. They do not come into being as the universe evolves; they were all there to start with; they precede the universe. I think Aquinas's view that the angels come into being along with the organisms that they're associated with makes better sense. Likewise, I think it makes better sense to think of the "laws of nature" as evolving habits rather than as eternal

---

59. ST 1, q. 61, a. 3

truths independent of the physical universe, as if in a transcendent mathematical mind.

Matthew: If we see the universe as a tiny pinprick in its beginning, how many angels would be around? Oh my, we're back to this question of how many angels could dance on a pinhead.

As the universe expands in size, does this mean that there's more work for angels, more room, more beings, more complex systems that angels could help govern?

If so, this might throw a lot of Aquinas's theory up in the air. His idea was that angels were created and then made their choice for good or evil, and nothing much has changed in the angelic realm since then, in terms of the quality of work that angels do.

Maybe the new prehistory is so unique that it's irreconcilable with the idea that all the angels were created at one time. This idea, one might say, is also a remnant of a Neoplatonic universe. As you were saying, as new galaxies are born and there's new work to do, does that mean that angels get birthed or created as well?

Rupert: It must. The present view of the universe is that as it expands, it cools down, and as it cools down, new forms of organization and order appear within it. In the context of an evolutionary cosmology, there would be an appearance of new angels all along. That would mean the continued creative activity of God would include the ongoing creation of new angels.

Matthew: And why not?

Rupert: There is also the question of what happens to angels when they are redundant. The angels that governed the dinosaurs don't have much to do now.

Matthew: Obviously they get recycled, or get training programs to govern the human beings.

Rupert: Or maybe evolution's occurring on other planets in the universe and they can simply be relocated. Dinosaur angels can move

THE PHYSICS OF ANGELS

in an instant to planets where dinosaurs are just coming into being and they can find useful work.

Matthew: Are there dinosaurs on other planets? I thought a species is a once-in-a-universe event. What brought the dinosaurs about was a pretty unique collection of happenings on this planet. It would be pretty difficult to repeat.

Rupert: Not if there's morphic resonance. The trillions of stars and trillions of planets may fall into species. Stars are already classified into several distinct types. There may be species of solar systems throughout the universe, and the planets within them may also fall into species. There may be dozens, hundreds, or even millions of planets that fall into the Mars species, or the Jupiter species, or the Earth species. If they're sufficiently similar, then there'd be morphic resonance among them. The evolutionary process on Earth would resonate with the evolutionary processes on other planets of the species Gaia.

The Raising Of The Angels To The State Of Grace And Glory

We have to understand that full and perfect bliss belongs by nature to God alone in whom to exist and to be happy are one and the same thing. In every creature, nature is one thing and perfect joy is another—this joy being the final end at which nature is aimed.[60] It is of the essence of bliss to be established or confirmed in goodness. By bliss is meant the ultimate perfection of a nature endowed with reason or intellect: which is why it is naturally desired. Everything has a natural desire for its ultimate perfection. ... The ultimate bliss which is beyond all natural capacities, this no angel had from the first moment of existence for it is not included in nature but is nature's goal. Hence the angels could not have had it from the beginning.[61] The angels

---

60. ST 1, q. 62, a. 4
61. ST 1, q. 62, a. 1

needed grace to turn to God so far as he is the object causing bliss. ... Angels have a natural love for God as source of their natural being; but we are speaking now of a turning towards God as source of the bliss that consists in seeing his essence unveiled.[62] Grace is a midway term between nature and glory.[63]

Matthew: For me the statement that "It is of the essence of bliss to be established or confirmed in goodness" is especially rich, because goodness is another word for blessing. So, here Aquinas is saying that bliss is about being established in blessing, both in an awareness of blessing and in an awareness of being blessed and of being an instrument of blessing. This is how bliss happens in the world.

When he says that everything has a natural desire for its ultimate completion and perfection, which is bliss, this is typical Aquinas. Desire is the motive of everything. Everything essentially seeks its own goodness and the goodness of the whole, the greater goodness. The good behind all goodness is divinity. And of course he's including angels in this cosmology of blessing and goodness.

He goes further when he talks about grace. Adding to this natural desire for God, grace is able to assist the unveiling of the divine essence. Grace is building on nature, even angelic nature, which by itself is not capable of experiencing the unveiled essence of divinity.

I think his recognition is that creatures, of any stripe, are not fully happy. There is a distinction between their existence and perfect happiness. Nature is one thing and perfect joy another, this joy being the final end. All creatures desire to increase their joy. Being, existence, and life are processes of increasing their experience of joy.

I think it's a surprise to read that. Most people probably don't think of God as being all that happy. But it puts divinity in a different

---

62. ST 1, q. 62, a. 2
63. ST 1, q. 62, a. 3

light: divinity is the most joyful. In another place Aquinas says, "God is most joyful and is therefore supremely conscious."[64] He connects consciousness and joy. And, of course, here he's talking about the immense joy of the angels.

Rupert: The Hindu conception of the ultimate divine consciousness is described as *satchidananda*—being-knowledge-bliss, indivisibly combined.

It's not clear to me exactly how Aquinas thinks of joy, and presumably you've thought about this because you've written a book, *Sheer Joy*, based on the writings of Aquinas. Is joy something that can only come through participation in something larger than oneself? If so, an angel or any created thing would have to go beyond itself in order to participate in it.

Matthew: Yes, I think Aquinas would put it that way. Definitely joy is never a private experience; it's part of a community experience. He even says, "Sheer joy is God's and this demands companionship."[65] Even the divine joy wants company with which to share the joy, wants community. Aquinas also plays with the Trinitarian motif that within divinity there is community and group joy. Then he extends that into creation itself. The community of creation is a receiver of divine joy and presumably a source of it as well.

Rupert: That makes it clearer as to why he thought angels, created in a state beyond anything we can imagine, need to go beyond their nature in order to achieve joy, and need grace to do so.

Were The Angels Created In Grace?

Though grace is midway between nature and glory in the ontological order, yet in the order of time it would not be appropriate for a creature to receive glory simultaneously with

64. Cited in Fox, *Sheer Joy*, 119.
65. Cited in Fox, *Sheer Joy*, 515.

its nature. For while glory is related to natural activities, aided by grace, as their outcome, grace itself is not related to them as an outcome. It does not result from them, but rather, on the contrary, they result from it, so far as they are good. And this is a ground for thinking that it was given to angels along with nature at the beginning.[66]

Matthew: To me this is a statement about what I would call original grace, original blessing. Angels were more blessed than other creatures. They received both their nature and their grace at the same time.

Rupert: What he seems to be saying is that the gap between natural activities and glory has to be bridged by grace. Grace has to come down from glory, as it were, and connect it with natural activities. Natural activities by themselves cannot reach out to glory; glory has to reach out to natural activities, and this reaching-out process involves grace.

Matthew: Yes. And there are other passages in Aquinas where he talks about the way that grace and nature both come from God. Grace is entirely a free gift of God, but so is nature. He's very careful not to create a dualism between nature and grace, as if nature is inferior and grace is to be set apart from nature. He is moving away from St. Augustine's separation of nature and grace, but he's not willing to be too explicit about it. Meister Eckhart, who came in the next generation and stood on Aquinas's shoulder, had the courage and directness to say, "Nature is grace."

Did Each Angel Obtain Bliss Immediately After One Meritorious Act?

Each angel obtained bliss immediately after meriting it with his first act of charity. ... It is characteristic of and proper to the angelic nature to reach its natural completeness in a single

---

66. ST 1, q. 62, a. 3

act, and not by a gradual process. ... It is consonant with the angel's nature that he goes immediately to the fullness of being appropriate to him.[67]

Matthew: This is certainly one area in which the angel was different from the human being. The angel had only one choice. As Aquinas says, the choice was one of charity. Those angels that we know as good angels made that choice, and from that moment on their nature was completed by grace and bliss, so they experienced its fullness all their lives long. This helps explain why they're filled with light and radiance, *doxa*, glory, and why encountering them awakens happiness in human beings.

Rupert: Aquinas elsewhere speaks about a succession of states in an angel (see page 103). Here it seems the first step they take is an act of charity that through grace links them to the source of bliss or joy. Thereafter, they remain in that state, but they can still change their knowledge according to what happens and have a succession of states of mind in time. Presumably, all those would be illuminated by bliss once they've made this first choice, and they would therefore communicate this bliss.

Is It Only By Pride And Envy That Angels Can Sin?

How can there be sin in desiring spiritual satisfactions? In one way only, namely by not observing the measure imposed by a higher will than one's own. And this precisely is the sin of pride—not to submit to one's superior where submission is due. Therefore the first sin in an angel can only have been pride. As a consequence, however, the angels could also sin by envy. For the same motive that draws you to desire something will make

---

67. ST 1, q. 62, a. 5

you detest the reverse of what you desire. Now envy consists of precisely in this, that one takes umbrage at another's wellbeing, as feeling it a hindrance to one's own. And so it was with the evil angel: he saw another's wellbeing as a hindrance to the possession of what he desired, and this just because he desired an unrivalled eminence which would no longer be such if another rose to eminence too. Therefore after the sin of pride he fell also into the evil of envy, detesting the wellbeing of mankind; and detesting too the majesty of God inasmuch as God makes use of man to further his own glory, against the devil's will.[68]

Rupert: Here we see the sin of pride as being the only one open to an angel originally, and then envy following from it. Are these not what Aquinas called the sins of the spirit? Other sins, such as lust and gluttony, depend on having bodies, so even devils would be immune from these.

Matthew: My understanding is that Aquinas includes among the sins of the spirit pride and envy but also avarice, *acedia*, despair, and fear. The mention of envy here is especially interesting. Pride and envy build one another up. Either the pride makes the envy worse or the envy makes the pride worse. Like the interconnectivity of things in the universe, there is an interconnectivity of spiritual sins.

Rupert: This is a theme developed by John Milton in his great poem *Paradise Lost*. He gives a wonderful portrayal of the fall of Satan through pride, and shows how the other fallen angels specialize in additional vices—avarice, for example, in the case of Mammon. What Aquinas is talking about here is worked out in immense detail by Milton in a most fascinating way.

Matthew: I think in our time the word *pride* is a problem because for politically oppressed people, it's always convenient to

---

68. ST 1, q. 63, a. 2

say that their sin is pride when they're trying to liberate themselves or achieve a measure of equality or justice. This abuse of the word *pride* by the powers-that-be has poisoned the word. I think a better translation today would be "arrogance." Pride itself is a virtue insofar as it's understood as self-esteem. Aquinas time and again teaches the need for self-love and how not to love oneself well is a sin; he talks about the self-love of angels too. In English the word *pride* has lost its real meaning as a sin of the spirit. The word *arrogance* gets the point across much better.

Rupert: I agree.

Matthew: Whereas envy is still alive and well. I don't think there's a saving side to the word *envy* as there is to the word *pride*.

Did The Devil Desire To Be As God?

The devil desired godlikeness in the sense that he placed his ultimate bliss in an objective to be obtained by the force of his own nature alone, rejecting the supernatural bliss which depends on the grace of God. Or if, perhaps, he did desire as his last end that likeness to God which is a gift of grace, he willed to possess this by his own natural power and not with the divine assistance in conformity to God's will. This would agree with Anselm's view that the devil desired that to which he would eventually have come had he curbed his desire.[69]

Matthew: Aquinas is not criticizing the devil or anyone else for desiring to be godlike. In fact, he says that this is not a sin. But the devil's desire to be godlike was a do-it-yourself divinity, a desire to do it by the force of his own nature alone, not with divine assistance. It was a sin of going it alone, not wanting to be a co-worker with God,

---

69. ST 1, q. 63, a. 3

even in the development of his own nature. It was a case of excessive reliance on his own powers to achieve a good end, but one that was not his own to achieve. There was a failure in cooperation, a failure in relatedness to the divine.

Rupert: I suppose there are many parallels in the human realm. One of them is the modern belief that humankind has outgrown the need for any notion of God or grace and can now seize control of its own, and the planet's, destiny. This has been the vision of secular humanism, and underlies the ideology of progress through science and technology. We're now seeing the bad sides of "progress," and faith in secular humanism is fading fast. It's now very difficult to believe that human reason alone, together with science and technology, can solve all the problems that confront us and bring about a brighter, better future on earth. The evidence seems to be against it.

The fullest embodiment of the belief that we can rely on our efforts alone was communism, whose ideology was based on the rational human control of everything, including human society, the economy, and nature. Materialism in its capitalist form involves a similar faith, although instead of everything being controlled by human planning, there is the belief that the market will bring it all about. This faith is not in God but in the market, in Mammon.

Matthew: Having come of age in the modern era, both systems share a belief in mechanism; somehow, if you get the mechanics of capitalism right or the mechanics of the communist system right, the machine will be self-oiling and will run successfully to everyone's advantage. Clearly this has not happened.

In some ways, that whole idea of mechanism comes close to Aquinas's naming of the devil's sin. If for "the force of his own nature alone … his own natural power" you substitute "the force of the machine alone … the machine's own power," that translates into the ideas of the marketplace and of communist bureaucracy.

Rupert: However, the devil at least acknowledged the existence and reality of God, whereas in modern secularism the very existence of God and grace is denied or ignored.

Matthew: I would say that for Karl Marx, much of his aspiration was about the biblical injunction of justice, and justice is one of the divine names. His was an effort to bring about justice in a very unjust moment in history, the burgeoning of the industrial society, with an excessive amount of power held in the hands of the few who owned factories, and the persecution of workers. He was lashing out against this injustice, which is a prophetic, biblical, and spiritual response. But certainly the praxis of his theories in the twentieth century, such as in the Soviet state, didn't conform to biblical norms of justice in the least. Today's fundamentalism linking up to big capitalism is equally scary.

When Did The First Angel Fall?

In all the angels the first act of self-reflection was good. But then some went on to turn to the Word with praise, while others remained in themselves, swollen with pride. Thus the first act was common to them all; it was by the second that they were separated. In a first instant they were all good; in a second, they divided into the good and the evil.[70]

Matthew: It's interesting in this passage how Aquinas pits praise against pride: that the good angels turn to praise, and the bad angels were swollen with pride, remaining in themselves. Praise is the act of not remaining in oneself; it's going out. I call praise the noise that joy makes. Praise is related to joy and it takes you out of yourself, and even beyond your own suffering.

---

70. ST 1, q. 63, a. 6

This reminds me of Meister Eckhart asking, "Who is a good person? A good person is one who praises good people." That's one more reason why envy is part of the sin of the devil, because envy is also a refusal to praise. It's a preoccupation with one's own desire for praise, wanting to be praised at the expense of others' right to praise.

Rupert: What do you think is the role of fallen angels in the nonhuman world? This is a big question. Is there evil in nonhuman nature? Is the entire cosmos good except for fallen angels and sinful people? Is the focus of Satan and fallen angels entirely concentrated on the human species or do they have other spheres of action too?

For example, would we expect to find devils behind some of the horrible things we see in the biological realm? Think of the ichneumon flies that lay eggs inside living caterpillars, and when the grubs hatch out they eat up the caterpillar from within. Do parasitism and disease represent diabolical principles?

Cancer, for example, represents an overstepping of the limits imposed by the higher order of the organism. Part of the organism becomes autonomous and grows in an uncontrolled way, at the expense of the good of the whole. Is this an expression of the satanic principle?

Are fallen angels at large in the universe, thinking up ever nastier diseases and more vicious forms of parasitism? Or do we see all those things as morally neutral, or even good in their own way, with evil spirits coming into play only in the human realm?

Matthew: Then there's the question of other beings, perhaps in other galaxies. If they have consciousness, then they must have choice, and if they have choice, are they subject to the sins of arrogance and envy?

Rupert: I think we have to conclude that this is likely. In the hierarchy or holarchy of nature, everything exists within a higher level of order, with limits to its autonomy. The tendency to break out of these limits must be an occupational disease of this kind of universe.

Therefore, we'd expect the same kinds of problems to arise in other conscious beings, whether they're humanlike or not.

Matthew: I'm reminded of two statements, one by Thomas Merton that "every non-two-legged creature is a saint," and the other by Rabbi Zalman Schachter, who says, "There is more good than evil in the world but not by much." Both Aquinas and Schachter stand in the biblical tradition that there's more grace and goodness than sin, but that doesn't mean that the sin is not real and that it's not powerful.

Rupert: According to Aquinas, angels were probably formed along with the corporeal universe (see page 113), and the second instant in their life involved the choice between good and evil. In the context of modern cosmology, the fall of the angels would have occurred very soon after the Big Bang. The first angels would have fallen within the first 10^{-30} seconds of the universe, or soon after.

What have the fallen angels been doing since then? Were devils putting a spoke in the wheel of galaxy, star, and planet formation right from the start?

Matthew: Since devils are envious, they'd be extremely envious of angels who have charge of governing these vast, beautiful, radiant systems. You'd think if they were at all spunky they would set out to disrupt, out of envy, the angels' potential success in making this universe a splendid place.

Rupert: If we take the view that new angels are created all the time as new galaxies, stars, planets, and species come into being, then in their second instant they have the choice between good and evil, according to Aquinas. This would mean, for example, that if the angel of a particular star chooses evil, that star would be under an evil influence. In traditional astrology there's the belief that certain stars are indeed of evil aspect, like Algol, the "demon star" in the constellation Perseus.

Matthew: It's all part of the cosmology. The Letter to the Ephesians says our struggle is against "cosmic powers, against the authorities and potentates of this dark age, against the superhuman forces of evil in the heavenly realms" (Ephesians 6,12). Human beings are not just struggling with our own inclination toward evil, but against demonic forces' inclination to evil in the heavens.

Rupert: This is very startling. We have grown used to thinking about the stars, the planets, and the sky as neither good nor evil, devoid of meaning, just following impersonal mathematical laws.

Was Satan The Highest Of All Angels Before He Fell?

In Ezekiel, Satan is addressed as a cherub. ... Cherubim is taken to mean "full of knowledge;" seraphim, "those on fire" or who "set on fire." The former name then denotes knowledge, which is compatible with mortal sin; the latter the ardour of charity, which is not. A reason for calling the first sinful angel a cherub rather than a seraph.[71] In the Bible, the names of two angelic orders, the Seraphim and the Thrones, are not given to devils; for they mean things incompatible with mortal sin, the ardour of charity and the presence of God. But devils are called Cherubim, Powers, and Principalities, since these terms denote knowledge and power, which are in the wicked as well as the good.[72] If we consider sin under the aspect of motive, it is clear that the greater angels were the more likely to fall: as we have seen, the diabolic sin was pride, and the motive of pride is eminence in nature.[73] As we have said already, when an angel moves to an objective, whether good or bad, he moves with all that is in him; there is nothing in him to slow him down. Hence the greatest angel,

---

71. ST 1, q. 63, a. 7
72. ST 1, q. 63, a. 9
73. ST 1, q. 63, a. 7

having greater natural power than the lesser angels, plunged into sin with correspondingly greater intensity. And this sufficed to make him the worst.[74]

Matthew: I am struck by this statement about the devil being a cherub, with "knowledge and power, which are in the wicked as well as the good." In the modern era there has been an explosion on humanity's part of both knowledge and power, for example, in the frightful military technology of nuclear and chemical weapons. I think being able to name knowledge and power as a latent place for demonic energy is very important.

Rupert: This connects us with the Faust story. In many ways the Faust myth is the myth of science. Faust sells his soul to the devil in return for unlimited knowledge and power.

Right from the beginning, the scientific enterprise was dedicated to knowledge and power. Even before the mechanistic revolution in the seventeenth century, Sir Francis Bacon was prophesying how a scientific priesthood dedicated to knowledge and power would transform humanity and the earth. The image of Faust selling his soul to the devil in return for knowledge and power sets out an archetypal pattern that underlies the entire mechanistic enterprise.

Of course, as Aquinas said, knowledge and power can be used for good. But if they are merely used to serve human ends, without any sense of God's power or grace, then this involves the satanic sin of arrogance.

Matthew: And the myth has been established that scientific knowledge is morally neutral. When scientists sell their power to military establishments, governments, and chemical companies, it doesn't take a doctoral degree in ethics to suspect that knowledge is not morally neutral. Like any other power, it requires spiritual discipline. It needs to be connected to justice and compassion and interdependence.

---

74. ST 1, q. 63, a. 8

We need to create contours for this tremendous power of knowledge that human science is capable of.

Another passage that moved me very much was this statement: "When an angel moves to an objective, whether good or bad, he moves with all that is in him; there is nothing in him to slow him down." I find that passage very exciting, very passionate. There's nothing in an angel to slow it down. If an angel's a species unto itself, it has no mother and father, no grandparents, no children to say, "Hey angel, you're off base here." It really is a power to itself, plunging in with all that is within it; with full intensity. I think that's a really interesting paragraph.

We have this notion of angels as ethereal beings that kind of float about and do pretty things and come around for pretty music and all. But here we have a statement from Aquinas about intensity and strength and latching on to a task and not letting go. This has a bright side to it. According to Aquinas, this is the way the good angels act too. So if angels are committed to see the universe run well, and the solar system run well, and this planet run well, it sounds like they'd be good beings to have on our side—genuinely intense and committed.

Rupert: I was also struck by the idea of Satan as a cherub. This sounds bizarre, because we have an image of cherubs as little boys with pink bottoms swarming over Baroque altarpieces. Aquinas reminds us that the cherubim are the highest, most powerful, and most frightening of all angels, not at all like little boys with wings. He gets us away from those grossly misleading images.

Matthew: Exactly. I also like his explanation of the seraphim being those on fire, those who set on fire, and identifying this with the ardor of charity. They are protected from sin by their very nature, whereas cherubim are more ambiguous. Knowledge and power can lead to mortal sin, but charity never does.

How Bad Angels Help

By their nature angels are between God and man. Now in the plan of divine providence the good of lower beings is achieved through higher beings. And the good of man is achieved in two ways. In the first place directly, in as much as we are drawn towards good and away from evil; and the suitable agents in this process are the good angels. And then also indirectly as when we are exercised in virtue by having to stand up to attacks and overcome opposition. And it is reasonable that this contribution to our wellbeing should be provided by the bad angels, lest after sinning they should cease to be of any use at all in the universe.[75]

Matthew: Aquinas is co-opting the bad angels—do what they will, they're making things better. This is not merely an abstract, theoretical statement from him, because at this time of his life, when he was writing the *Summa Theologiae*, he was under tremendous opposition, being attacked on the one hand by the secular Aristotelians, the atheists if you will, and on the other hand by fundamentalists, who were very vocal. I sense that this is a personal statement from him. Being attacked and overcoming opposition exercises our virtue. And virtue, for Aquinas, is the whole basis of morality His morality is not based on commandments, but on virtues, which signify a positive development of power, healthy power. Good angels are supporting us and bad angels are still being useful, because they help us build up our virtuous muscles.

Rupert: And it recalls the old idea that each person has a good angel and a bad angel. We see this, for example, in Christopher Marlowe's play *Doctor Faustus*. When Faust is deliberating whether to sell his soul to the devil, on one side of the stage stands his good angel and on the other his bad angel, both offering their advice. The bad

---

75. ST 1, q. 64, a. 4

angel prevails. This way of representing the drama of good and evil personalizes it. We have not only a good angel assigned to us, but a bad angel as well, and both come to bear on our moral decision making.

Matthew: This raises the question of mystery and wisdom. To counterbalance the bad angels of unremitting knowledge, power, and arrogance, we need angels of wisdom today. Wisdom is never anti-intellectual. It never puts down knowledge, but it puts it in its larger context of love—justice and service and heart. And of the divine wisdom, a connection to divinity.

The loss of mystery in the modern era is part of the shadow side of knowledge running around naked, looking for its power place, and not looking for wisdom. We have committed reductionism on mystery. Many people think when they hear the word *mystery*, it just means those scientific laws that we have not yet discovered, it's just a lacuna in our knowledge. But that's not what mystery means. Mystery is that dimension to reality that we encounter but do not alter.

It seems to me that everything connected to the divine is mysterious. Aquinas has a great line: "We will never know the essence even of a single fly." The fly guards its essence. He also mentions this in his study on angels when he says that the angel can never know our mystery. We keep our secret, the secret of our essence.

And if this is true of a fly, or us, or an angel, imagine how true it is of all beings taken together, of the whole collective of the cosmos, to say nothing of the source of all things, the divine mystery.

Part of our being cut off from the God-force in the quest for knowledge, power, and arrogance is being cut off from the mystery. There's a great sadness in that. To live life only at the level of problem-solving may miss what living life is really about. Life is much more about living in mystery than about conquering mystery or just problem-solving. And among the mysteries are the angels, still, even after all this.

Rupert: They are more mysterious than ever. In the Middle Ages people thought they'd got angelology more or less worked out. They knew the hierarchies, and how the different orders of the angels fitted into their cosmology. They adapted their understanding of the angels very well to the prevailing geocentric cosmology.

Since then we've had several centuries when angels have been regarded by many intellectuals as figurative or symbolic figures at best. Many people neither believe in the bad nor in the good angels. But if the fallen angels are for real, they must be having a wonderful time. I suppose the bad angels can function very effectively when no one even suspects they're there.

We now have a completely different, vastly larger, and much more creative cosmology than they had in the Middle Ages. The angels of such a cosmos are very mysterious indeed. We have hardly begun to try to understand how their conscious powers may be related to the evolution of nature, to the development of humanity, or to the expansion of human consciousness. We know next to nothing about the superhuman intelligences that influence our lives for good and ill.

Hildegard of Bingen

Hildegard of Bingen (1098-1179) was an extraordinarily gifted person whose life practically spanned the extraordinarily creative twelfth century in the West. That century brought us Chartres Cathedral, the invention of the university, and the introduction of a new cosmology that arrived via Islamic translations of Aristotle. Hildegard was a Benedictine abbess in the Rhineland area of Germany, where she was famous in her lifetime for her writings (she authored ten books on subjects ranging from holistic health to plants, trees, rocks, and fish, plus theology, cosmology, and science); her healing; her paintings; and her music (she composed, among other works, the first opera of the West, and her Gregorian chant is unique). She was also the poet and lyricist for her musical compositions. In addition to being a mystic, Hildegard was a prophet, calling church leaders to reform and renewal both in her letter writing and in her preaching, which she undertook in major cathedrals and monasteries of her day.

Angels play an important role in Hildegard's personal experience and in her cosmology and theology. We have chosen the following selections from her writings on angels both for their interest and because they are representative of her angelology.

God As The Source Of The Angelic Fire

The original fire out of which the angels burn and live, that is God himself. This fire is every glory out of which the mystery of mysteries comes forth.[76] The angels surround God in their glowing fire, for they are living light. They do not have wings like birds but are still hovering flames in the power of God.[77] God is the original living source who sent out the waves. When he spoke the words, "Let it be," there existed illuminating beings.[78] Their nature is a glowing burning. They burn from God, who is the root of the fire. Through no other can they be enflamed or extinguished. In love of God this fire burns inextinguishably.[79]

Rupert: Hildegard sees fire as the source of the angels, the fire of God. In the context of modern cosmogony, with its primal fireball, this is an amazing image.

Matthew: She is saying that, just as light was the first creation, as depicted in Genesis 1, so these light-beings, illuminating beings, were birthed at the same moment. Like us today, she is connecting the angels to her cosmogony; and since hers is based quite strictly on the Bible, she is linking the first creation with the coming of the angels. Her language is so vivid. The angels don't just come to be; they burn and live, according to her. God is the original fire. Glory, *doxa*, is a word for the divine radiance.

Angels don't really have wings like birds, but are more like flames hovering in the power of God. This image of Hildegard's really shifts our image of what an angel looks like.

---

76. Hildegard of Bingen, *Liber Vitae Meritorum* (Pitra, 1882), 24.
77. Hildegard of Bingen, *Wisse die Wege Scivias* 111, 4.
78. Hildegard of Bingen, J. P Migne, ed. *Patrologia Latina* (PL) (Paris: Migne,1844-91), 197, 229C.
79. PL 197, 262D.

Light And Mirroring

[God says:] "I have created mirrors to look upon my face, to observe all of the never-ending wonders of my origins. I have prepared for myself these mirror beings to join in songs of praise. Through my word, which without beginning was and is in me, I let a powerful light go forth in these innumerable hosts, the angels."[80]

And God created light, invisible illumination which clings to the living, flying spheres: the angels.[81]

Oh you angels, whose being streams out from your countenance. You alone glimpse the most internal power of creation which the father's heart breathes. You see it as in a face.[82]

[The angels are] a light on which the spheres of life would depend.[83]

Rupert: Hildegard goes further than saying that the angels are reflections or mirrors; light streams out through them, and the spheres of light depend on them. They are now intermediaries as well as mirrors. In a sense, they are two-way mirrors. They reflect back to God. God is seeing the Godself in the mirror of the angels. At the same time they are intermediaries, transmitting the light of God into the realms of life.

Matthew: When Hildegard says, "God created light, invisible illumination," she shows this is not like the light of the sun, for the sun did not yet exist. In our cosmogony, too, the sun is not nearly as old as the universe. We usually think of light as the light that the sun gives, but that's not her notion of the origin of light, nor is it the

---

80. PL 197, 889A.
81. PL 197, 917B.
82. *Liber Vitae Meritorum*, 444.
83. PL 197, 917B.

contemporary notion. Probably we have to imagine a different kind of light experience from that of the sun, which is impossible.

Rupert: Maybe it's not impossible. Through physics we know of many forms of invisible radiation. Visible light is but a small part of the electromagnetic spectrum. Radio astronomers pick up radio waves from distant galaxies. And the cosmic microwave background radiation all through the universe is the fossil light from the Big Bang, according to current cosmology.

The vast majority of the electromagnetic spectrum is invisible to our eyes because of the limitations of eyes. What is visible has more to do with the nature of eyes than with the nature of radiation itself. All forms of electromagnetic radiation involve photons.

If angels are transmitters of light, visible and invisible, that which streams out from them includes ultraviolet and infrared light, cosmic rays, radio waves, microwaves, and X-rays. They are involved in the vast complex of radiation that interconnects the whole creative cosmos and that also links humanity together on Earth through electromagnetic technologies such as radio and television.

Cosmic Praise

Just as sunshine shows the sun, so also angels announce God through their praise, and just as the sun cannot exist without its light, so also the Godhead is nothing without the angels' praise.[84]

The entire cosmos sang the song of the angels.[85]

In wonderful harmonics the angels announce in high song the glorification of God. In indescribable jubilation the blessed spirits through God's power exalt the wonders which he works. The song of joy and blessedness rules throughout the heavens.[86]

---

84. PL 197, 746C.
85. *Liber Vitae Meritorum*, 157.
86. PL 19 7, 442A.

The angels' tongues are simply pure praise. ... And so the fire has its flames and it is praise before God. And the wind moves the flames: in order to praise God. And in the voice lives the word: that is also a praise of God. And a voice will be heard. And that also is pure praise for God. Therefore the entire world is praise of God.[87]

Matthew: It's interesting how necessary Hildegard sees praise to be in the universe and indeed in divinity. Praise is a response to beauty, to grace, to joy. She's saying that praise lies at the heart of the Godhead. As light is to the sun, praise is to God.

Rupert: The angels' tongues are pure praise. Fire is also praise, the flickering flames are praise. Voice is praise, hearing is praise. All these images of praise are images of movement; fire moves, wind moves, tongues move, breath moves, hearing moves. In this praise there is a reverse movement toward God, perhaps a mirroring. Energy moves out from God through the angels, and this movement back toward God in the form of praise is vibratory, dynamic, and meaningful.

Matthew: These texts also demonstrate the cosmological context in which Hildegard operates and in which the angels operate. She says, "The entire world is praise of God." And she says that "The entire cosmos sang the song of the angels." Song and praise are coming forth from the entire universe.

This is not about individual voices; it's about a cosmic vibration, a cosmic song, cosmic waves, praise. Just as our eyes can only pick up limited amounts of light, so the implication is that our ears are only picking up a limited amount of song. And fire, and wind. The secret word hidden in things is offering a universal and constant praise to God.

Rupert: All this praise is seen in terms of vibration. Sound is vibratory, flickering flames are vibratory. We now think scientifically of

---

87. *Liber Vitae Meritorum*, 352.

all nature as vibratory. Everything is rhythmic, oscillatory, even down to the heart of the atom.

But in what sense could vibratory activity in the universe praise God? And if God hears praise of a vibratory or sonorous nature, then how does he hear it? He does not hear with ears, but perhaps our ears can provide an analogy. How does hearing work? It works by resonance. The eardrum vibrates. It resonates with whatever sound you're hearing. To hear sound, you have to have a resonant mode of responding.

This suggests that the sensorium of God, through which this praise is experienced, must be essentially resonant in nature. Otherwise, praise in voices and sound and vibration would be unheard and unseen by God. And any response must involve resonance.

Matthew: And what exactly do we mean by resonance? A passage to receive vibration?

Rupert: It's not just a matter of receiving vibration, but also of responding to it. The classic image is the sympathetic resonance of stretched strings. I like hearing the sympathetic resonance of pianos. If you lift the lid, press down the sustaining pedal, and chant "ooo" into the piano, it will say "ooo" back to you. If you chant "aaa" into a piano on the same note as before, the piano will say "aaa" back. These vowel sounds differ in their pattern of overtones, and the different strings responding to these overtones resonate to give the vowel sound back. This is like the image of the mirror transposed into the realm of sound.

Just as our eyes respond only to a limited spectrum of light, our ears respond only to a limited range of frequencies, and microphones respond only to a limited range of frequencies. But if the whole universe is praising God and if God can hear that praise, he must respond to it, which implies a capacity to resonate at all frequencies and in all places.

Matthew: A word is that which vibrates, and it also reveals. Every creature is being heard by God and, as you say, God is vibrating with every creature. There is a sense of communion and of equality between divine hearing and praising. That sustains what Hildegard says: "In the voice lives the word." The word will be heard. In the modern era we have succeeded in anthropocentrizing the word *word*. Yet in truth "word" is much more primal, and to reunderstand it as vibration helps us to deanthropocentrize divinity.

Rupert: Does praise need to be conscious? Atoms vibrate and the divine sensorium may resonate with their vibration, but is this in itself a form of praise? Since angels are conscious beings, presumably their praise is at a different level from that of the rest of creation.

Matthew: Yet Hildegard is saying fire praises and wind praises. She's not saying they just give out sound or vibration.

Rupert: How do you make sense of that?

Matthew: The elements, by doing what they're here to do, by being true to themselves, are praising because they've certainly come to construct something praiseworthy, which is to say the beauty and the order and the implicit purpose of the universe. Maybe there's conscious praise and unconscious praise.

Rupert: But praise implies a conscious awareness of what's being praised. Praise for beauty implies an awareness of ugliness. Praise for light implies an awareness of darkness, and so on. It seems to me that praise has to have this element of consciousness and choice.

Matthew: The key there is the word *choice*. That there are beings that can choose not to praise or to praise. And perhaps that's the difference between what we call the elements that praise and the angels and human beings that praise. The fire and the wind are perhaps praising unconsciously, they are not choosing not to praise. Whereas human beings are capable of choosing things other than praise, such as cynicism, self-pity, and being too wrapped up in themselves to observe the grace and beauty around them.

Good Works

And just as God is praised by the angels and as his creation is acknowledged through this praise, for they sound his praise with zithers and harmony and all voices of praise, because this is their actual office, so also God is to be praised by humanity. For humans serve two purposes: they sing God's praise and they practice good works. So God is recognised through their praise, and through the good works one can see in them God's wonders.

So humans are angelic through their praise (laus), but through their holy deeds (opus) they are human. But as a whole they are the full work of God (plenum opus Dei), for in praise and in deeds all of God's works are brought to completion through these humans.[88]

Matthew: Hildegard is saying that the *via positiva*, which is praise, is half our task. We share that with the angels. The other half of our task is action. Hildegard is providing a very balanced picture of humanity here. We are here both to praise and to work, and the best work flows from our praise—action from nonaction, as it were.

Rupert: But it's not clear to me what the distinction is between praise and work. Angels not only praise, they also have work to do: for example, they are messengers. When Hildegard says the characteristic of humanity is a potential for holy deeds, does this mean that the choice between good and bad goes on all the time for human beings? For the angels, this choice existed only at the beginning, according to the traditional view. Some angels fell, but the ones that didn't fall never lose their connection with God. Everything they do is in God's service, not only praising God but also in harmony with each other. The musical metaphor, and particularly the use of the word harmony, implies that

---

88. *Liber Vitae Meritorum*, 217.

not only are they relating to God, but they're relating to each other. Harmony depends on interrelationship.

Matthew: Exactly. This is the difference that she sees between the angels and the humans. The angels make one eternal choice for praise, but human beings have to make this on a daily basis. And praise is larger than work, because within praise the angel works. But the human creature has to choose to work. This has implications for the nature of creativity. Human beings are creative and angels aren't. They've only made one choice, and that's it. Our creativity is a choice we have to make daily. We have to struggle to bring together our work and choices with a consciousness of praise.

One way to see the difference between praise and work is in terms of the *via positiva* (which is praise) and the *via transformativa* (which puts praise to work through our creativity).

Angels Move as Fast as Thought

Angels do not have wings as birds do, but fly many times as fast, at the same pace that human thoughts travel.[89]

Rupert: We are used to the image of angels with wings, and it is a very ancient image, found in many traditions. There are winged spirits in shamanism; in Egypt, Babylon, and Sumeria; in Hinduism and Buddhism and in traditions all over the world. These are presumably related to the speed and freedom of movement of birds, to the experience of flying in our dreams, and to the shamanic experience of flying in trance.

But here Hildegard is saying that this is simply an image; it's an indication of the fact that they can move very fast. Flight is the most free and rapid form of movement. So the wings of angels shown

---

89. *Liber Vitae Meritorum*, 75.

in so many pictures are really an image of the capacity for free and rapid movement. Hildegard is going beyond that common image: angels move as fast as thought. Even today, that is the best metaphor. We don't know how fast thoughts travel. If I telephone somebody in Australia I can transmit a thought to that person at the speed of light. But maybe thoughts can move even faster than this. If I look at a distant star, there's a sense in which my thoughts reach out to touch that star, moving over literally astronomical distances with the utmost speed.

Matthew: When I hear you speak this way, my feelings are of hope. There are beings in the universe that can accomplish things very rapidly. And we're among them. We can, as you say, speak and image things almost at the speed of light.

This gives hope that we can change thought for the better, not just for the worse, at a speed that will heal our bodies and minds in time to be praisers of life and the planet instead of destroyers.

Rupert: In the human realm, this question of whether or not thoughts can move faster than the speed of light is not a big issue. You would need measuring instruments with a sensitivity of microseconds to be able to detect whether a thought transmitted telepathically can reach Australia before a telephone call. But it becomes an interesting question in relation to the angels in the cosmos. Our galaxy, for example, is about 100,000 light-years across. So an angelic thought, if it moves at the speed of light, would take 100,000 years to reach from one side of the galaxy to the other.

Matthew: Well, that's very important. The expanded size of the universe, I think, makes for more legions of angels being put to work. I know there's a woman in Switzerland who experiences angels, and she says it takes them four or five days to get here.

Rupert: From where?

Matthew: From wherever they hang out. She hears them coming, and they come singing music and they teach her these songs that she writes down, even though she's not a musician. But she hears them coming and it takes them four or five days to arrive.

Rupert: If they traveled at the speed of light, they would be pretty local ones. The nearest star to the solar system is four light-years away, and many of the stars we see in the sky are hundreds of light-years away. Communication at the speed of light with spirits linked to those stars would take many times longer than a human lifetime, and for more distant stars, longer than the whole history of civilization. So if there is any form of communication back and forth between us and distant stars and galaxies, it must be faster than the speed of light.

Matthew: So there are a lot of angels out there that we are never going to meet in this lifetime.

Rupert: It does rather depend on the velocity of angelic thought, which Hildegard leaves open. And the question's just as open today. We can't say there have been fundamental advances in the understanding either of angelic movement or of the speed of thought since Hildegard's day.

Matthew: But because there have been advances in terms of the size of the universe, the question has been extended.

Rupert: Yes, it becomes a more pressing question, more relevant rather than less so.

Hierarchical Order

For God, the all powerful, sets the heavenly hosts into various orderings according to the divine will. Some of these orderings are meant to practice special services, but each of them is meant to be a mirror-ordering of the seals of each other. In each of these reflections lie hidden mysteries which each angelic ordering cannot completely see or know or sense or bring to completion. For this reason they wait in amazement and climb from praise to praise and continually renew themselves in this way, and their praise will never be exhausted.[90]

Rupert: The hierarchical ordering of angels is something that everybody who's written on angels seems to agree about, although the details differ. Like Dionysius and Aquinas, Hildegard recognizes nine orders, arranged in concentric circles. They are in a nested hierarchy or holarchy.

Matthew: What we see here is a rounding of the word hierarchy in Hildegard. She also said, "God is a wheel." The nested hierarchy is essential because interdependence is essential; the various orders need one another, just as the parts need the whole and the whole needs the parts in any structure. This is nice because it brings angels into a natural sphere. It doesn't make them a law unto themselves; rather, they seem to follow the same patterns of interconnectivity between the whole and the parts that the rest of nature follows.

Rupert: That would necessarily be so. There's no way that angels could function as governing consciousnesses independently of the order in which the things they govern are arranged.

Matthew: And I like her phrase about hidden mysteries in each of these relationships.

Rupert: Such mysteries are at every level in a holarchical order. For example, there are things a liver cell can never comprehend about the whole liver, and things the liver cannot comprehend about the entire organism, such as you or me.

Matthew: Isn't it true too that the individual organism can never comprehend everything there is to know about a cell?

Rupert: Yes. Our comprehension is related to the level at which we work. We can study the organization of a cell through cell biology and biochemistry, but to get inside a cell, to discern the awareness of a cell, is beyond our understanding because it works in a completely

---

90. PL 197, 960D-961A.

different way. It's obviously not going to be speaking English, and not going to be preoccupied with its income tax and that kind of thing. A cell has other concerns. They're not ours. Between every level there is relationship but also a mutual incomprehensibility.

An important aspect of the holarchy of angels is the awareness that there are many levels of consciousness other than the human. This is denied by materialists and secular humanists, who look on the whole of nature as unconscious, blind mechanism. Out of the primal slime life crawled forth, and in the fullness of time mammals emerged, and then human consciousness and reason appeared. This is the only form of consciousness in the whole of nature. There is no divine mind and no angels, although there may be humanoids on other planets with science like ours. But the idea of different levels or orders of consciousness is not present in the modern secular worldview. What an incredible impoverishment that is!

Matthew: And how arrogant and anthropocentric. Yet we claim that the Copernican revolution moved us away from a human-centered world to an objective view of the universe, but in many ways what's happened since has become duller, less mysterious, less imaginative, and more human-centered than anything our ancestors believed before Copernicus.

Rupert: And it's actually called "humanism," putting humans at the center.

Matthew: Now that we see the universe is so large, isn't it almost silly to think that this tiny realm of humanity is the only seat of consciousness and reason in the universe? Isn't it almost an absurdity?

Rupert: Yes. And yet this is often portrayed as an enlightened understanding. In many ways the Enlightenment narrowed consciousness by focusing on human reason, our very limited capacity for understanding.

Matthew: Perhaps what humanists were really saying is that we're the only ones with books. And maybe they're right. If angels and spirits can travel at the speed of thought, then maybe they are far more in the thought realm than we are. And they don't need as many media as we do to get there.

Rupert: Exactly—they don't need the Internet.

Darkness

[God said:] "I, who am at home in all the ends of the world, revealed my work in the East, the South, and the West. But the fourth quarter in the North I left empty; neither sun nor moon shines there. For this reason in this place, away from all worldly structures, is hell, which has neither a roof above nor a floor below. Here it is where pure gloom reigns, but this gloom simultaneously stands in service to all of the lights of my fame. How namely could light be recognised if not through the darkness? And how would one know the gloom if not through the radiating splendour of my servants of light? If this were not so, then my power would not be perfect; for not all of my wondrous deeds could be described."[91]

Rupert: This is a fascinating passage from several points of view. First, it states that the creation of light necessarily involves the creation of darkness, the separation of light from darkness. And this is the very nature of light as we understand it. Light involves a polarity of light and darkness. The wave motion of light leads to alternating patches of light and darkness when two beams of light interfere with each other. Light is made up of waves. One side is light, the other darkness. And as Hildegard says, darkness is necessary for light to be recognized. All perception depends on contrast.

---

91. PL 197, 812B.

When she says that the empty space was in the north, she's using our experience as the basis of her metaphor. In the Northern Hemisphere, the sun and the moon and the planets don't shine in the north. There are stars in the north, of course, such as the Polestar. But this is a local metaphor based on our experience rather than an absolute principle. In Australia, for example, one of the most disconcerting features is the way that the midday sun is in the north. The sun never shines in the south.

The deeper meaning of the metaphor is that when we look out into the night sky, beyond and around all the heavenly bodies is blackness. Darkness is very much part of the universe as we experience it.

Matthew: It's telling that she sets this discussion of darkness in the cosmological context of the four directions. Among Native Americans, the north usually stands for wildness; when you pray to the spirits of the north, you pray for strength of heart to endure the long nights, wild winds, and darkness. When you pray to the south, you're praying for the spirit of kindness and gentleness, because that's where the sun comes from.

Her picture of hell is not that of fire, but of coldness. As Dante a century later would say, the real depths of hell are ice and not fire. The ultimate depths are ice.

She's not afraid to look to the north, to look to the dark for what it has to teach us. And what's clear is that the Creator made all four directions, including the darkness. But the darkness, she says, stands in service to all of the lights. So darkness serves light, and light serves darkness.

In the theological tradition this is a celebration of the apophatic divinity, God in the darkness. This distinguishes Hildegard from a lot of New Agers who, it seems to me, often avoid that dimension of the north, the dimension of the shadow and darkness. They tend to see the world dualistically, saying that darkness is not worthy of us, or that it is evil, or that only light exists. In fact, darkness is one of our teachers too. The mystics talk about this plunge into the darkness as the *via negativa*.

Hildegard is honoring the important and positive role that darkness plays, talking about the darkness of the womb and the darkness before birth, gestation in times of gloom, of doubt and of waiting. The womb is a place of positive fecundity, though it be dark.

Rupert: The fact that she calls it hell shows that hell is not principally evil or bad, it's simply the dark realm. Early conceptions of hell were of the underworld, weren't they? It was dark, but not necessarily bad.

Matthew: That's very Jewish. Sheol, like Hades, is a place of unknowability more than of punishment. But she says it has neither roof nor floor. Does that mean it's infinite out there?

Rupert: Presumably it corresponds to the darkness, the vastness of space.

Matthew: And also to the vastness of the dark area of the soul where you feel there is no floor when you're sinking into real pain, real suffering, real grief. Grief has no roof and no floor. It feels infinite, as if it will never end.

Lucifer

In the first angel God drew all of the beauty in the works of his omnipotence. God decorated him as a heaven and as an entire world: with all of the stars and the beauty of verdure and all types of glittering stones. And he called him Lucifer, light-bearer, because he carried the light from him who alone is eternal.[92]

This one, though he must have perceived that he only had to serve God with his beautiful ornamentation, separated himself from God's love and went towards the darkness, in which he began to speak to himself: "What majestic thing it would be if

---

92. PL 197, 812B.

I could act according to my own will and perform deeds which I have seen only God do?" His supporters agreed with him and called out: "Yes we want to place the throne of our master in the North against the all-highest."[93]

Pride germinated in the first angel as he looked upon his own radiance, and in his conceit he no longer comprehended the source of this light. And so he spoke to himself, "I want to be master and I do not want anyone over me." Instead his majesty slipped away and was forfeited: so he became the prince of hell.[94]

Matthew: Lucifer is the first created being and bears in himself great beauty and great light. But as a being of consciousness, he had a decision to make. That decision is about praise or no praise. As Hildegard puts it, his arrogance germinated on his own radiance and his conceit. He no longer comprehended the source of the light and beauty that was his.

Hildegard is describing Lucifer's choice, his sin, as a refusal to praise and a refusal to look to the source of his own beauty. That's why I prefer the word *arrogance* to *pride*. I think one needs pride; pride is the ability to see beauty in oneself. Arrogance is a refusal to see the origin and the cause of the beauty. I think arrogance is the abrogating to oneself the source of one's being and existence in light and beauty. That is absurd, especially in an evolutionary universe, because we are all products of what has come before.

I see Lucifer's sin, as described by Hildegard, as very much at the forefront of human perversity today. So much of our unwillingness to relate peacefully and joyously and justly with other humans and other beings is our refusal to see the common source that we share.

---

93. PL 197, 812B.
94. PL 197, 170A.

To lay sin at the feet of a refusal to look at one's origins is to underline the capital importance of the creation story. This is where our morality comes from. It was Lucifer's refusal to look at his own creation story that turned his healthy pride into sinful arrogance. I think there's a lesson here for us today We need a story of origins and an honoring of the source and a praising of the source, lest we too turn healthy pride into sinful arrogance.

Rupert: Any part depends on the whole. Everything depends on its larger source and environment. And any created being depends on its relationship with the source of creation and the rest of creation for its existence.

This lack of concern with the whole, with the environment on which we depend, is at the root of our ecological problems too. It is sheer arrogance to believe that we can own and use what this earth provides with no regard for the source, and with no regard for the greater living context in which we exist.

The fall of Lucifer happens at the very beginning of creation, long before the creation of the rest of the universe. Right from the start there's this separation. Maybe this is in the nature of things. Just as the formation of light involves the formation of darkness, so the formation of a consciousness with free will must involve the exercise of that free will in the denial of its source. Only when that choice is made is the polarity of the choice made real.

The origin of consciousness, God-created consciousness, is in the consciousness of Lucifer, the most splendid of all the angels and the first. The exercise of this free will in claiming autonomy, refusing to recognize the source, is right there at the beginning of consciousness. This may be the primary polarity in consciousness, to praise or to deny the source.

The first acts of creation, according to Genesis 1, established the primary polarities, first of all, the polarity of darkness and light.

According to Hildegard, as well as Dionysius and Aquinas, with the light is created the consciousness of the angels. Immediately after that, Lucifer made his choice, and polarity was established within created consciousness, the polarity manifested in arrogance and praise. The polarity of moral lightness and darkness was the second thing in creation.

Matthew: This is very like the Adam and Eve story and the symbol of the tree of good and evil. With the first human consciousness there was choice, and the first human beings, like Lucifer, chose to ignore the source. Yet unlike Lucifer, it was not a once-only decision, because human beings have many, many options. We learn by trial and error.

Yes, I think that just as light, the first thing created, contains within itself waves of darkness, so our yearning for good and our own goodness, our own blessing, contains within itself the capacity for moral darkness. And this polarity seems inevitable, just as in a universe with light darkness is intrinsic.

Rupert: Hildegard says that Lucifer "separated himself from God's love and went towards the darkness, in which he began to speak to himself." This movement into the darkness allowed a differentiation of his own consciousness, an internal dialogue. And the internal dialogue encourages pride and envy.

Darkness already exists. Lucifer's movement into darkness is the first step. The internal dialogue then begins.

Matthew: And Hildegard says he started by saying, "I want to be master and I do not want anyone over me." In terms of the cosmology we were talking about earlier, he has cut himself off from what you call the hierarchical nesting, the relationship of interdependence with God and the rest of creation. Again, this is a very modern problem. Descartes promised that we would be masters of nature. Our "fall" has been in terms of our willful ignorance of our roles of interdependence with the rest of creation. Thomas Berry calls our talking to ourselves the autism of the modern world, our willfully chosen isolation and rugged independence, our master-slave relationship with the rest of nature, and even a closing down of our own feelings, of our own bodies and minds, instead of opening up to the wonders of interrelationship, of the cosmos and the splendors of its many beings. All this seems to be a repeat of Lucifer's solipsism and autism.

Envy

"Every creation of God radiates"—so he screams enviously —"and none of it shall be mine!"[95]

Rupert: Hildegard imagines the thoughts of Lucifer as he looks back from the darkness into the rest of creation. Now that he is separated, envy comes into play. Here we have an actual sequence in which deadly sins evolve. Arrogance comes first and it's rapidly followed by envy.

Matthew: Arrogance is an attitude toward oneself and envy is a response to others. They're closely related because when one does not see oneself in the context of interdependence with the greater community, then one wants to seize what the others have. There is not the natural give-and-take that happens within a community that loves one another.

It's like Jesus saying, "Love others as you love yourself." Lucifer's really saying, "Hate and envy others as you're misloving yourself," which is what arrogance is—it's a misloving, a distorted love.

There's no concept here of creativity. Lucifer is not saying, "Maybe I can share with the other creatures their beauty," or "Maybe

---

95. *Liber Vitae Meritorum*, 36 1.

together we can create a new situation where there's enough for all of us." He has no way out. Creativity is not an option for angels as it is for us. An angel from this point of view is not really an evolutionary being. It has only one choice to make. All the other beings, at least as species if not as individuals, are in the habitual process of adapting, creating, changing.

The Abyss

Because Lucifer with his followers proudly scorned to recognise God, the blazing radiance with which the power of God had adorned him died within him. He himself destroyed the beauty within him, the recognition of which should have served him to the good. And greedily he stretched himself towards evil which pulled him into its abyss. In this way the eternal majesty was extinguished for him and he plummeted into perpetual corruption. The remaining stars also became black like extinguished coals. With their seducer they were disrobed of the majestic radiance. They extinguished in gloomy perdition, deprived of every light of bliss, as coals which lack the spark of fire.

And forthwith a whirlwind drove them out and hunted them from the South to the North, behind him who sat on the throne. They plummeted into the abyss and you will see none of them again.

The wind's bride of godlessness whirled the angels of evil high because they wanted to elevate themselves above God and bring God down through their pride. It blew them into the bitterness of black corruption. It tore them away from the South and the good and pulled them backwards into the past. For God, who rules over everything, they are no more.[96]

---

96. *Scivias* 111, 1.

Rupert: This is an astonishing passage about the way the fallen angels are whirled into darkness. I'm intrigued by the way the other stars, the angels who follow Satan, become black. Their light goes out. No light can come from them. And they go into an abyss of darkness.

Hildegard invites us to look for cosmological parallels by talking of stars, and two forms of darkness seem relevant. One is the darkness of space itself, which is very cold and very dark and without radiance. To be lost in interstellar space must be a pretty terrible fate. Nothing much happens. It's a dismal place to be in.

The second kind of darkness is that of black holes. Black holes are the remains of stars that have collapsed in on themselves. Their gravitational pull is so strong that nothing can come out of them: not even light can escape from them. Black holes give us a modern metaphor for this state of being of an entity so turned in on itself, so drawn in by its own gravity, and so strongly self-centered that nothing whatsoever can come out. All it can do is suck other things into itself. A black hole is like a drainpipe in the universe, down which things go and out of which nothing can come. As far as we're concerned, once things have gone into them they are no more. This gives a much more graphic vision of perdition, of total loss, than the usual old-fashioned images of hell. Who would want to be cast into the abyss of a black hole?

Matthew: Right. There's no possibility of creativity and of new life, and that's why for God the fallen angels are no more, because God is where there is life. All light of bliss has been extinguished. There is no spark of fire, as Hildegard says.

She is combining cosmology with morality. The wind tore the fallen angels from the south and the good, and pulled them backward to the past. This is apocalyptic language; cosmological happenings have psychological and moral implications. She brings together psyche and cosmos.

As you say, the cosmology of black holes today, like Hildegard's cosmology of cold black places, gives us powerful metaphors for naming not just moral states but psychic experiences. We can plunge into dark holes of sterility, despair, depression, loneliness, alienation.

From this point of view, hell is not something that happens after death. We are pulled into it in the course of our psychic journey, in our spiritual lives. This corresponds with a cosmology that recognizes that there are spaces out there that not even God can touch. We're talking at three levels here: cosmology, morality, and psychology, the journey of the soul on the *via negativa*.

Human Beings Replace The Fallen Angels

At this time God formed another life form. He sunk this life into bodies and had it elevate itself. And that is the humans. Now God gives them the place and the honour of the lost angels so that the humans could complete the praise which the angels did not want to do. Some with this human countenance are characterised by devotion to the world in their corporeal works. But in their spiritual senses they constantly serve God. In spite of their worldly duties they never forget their spiritual service to God. And these faces are turned towards the East. That is where the origin of holy transformation and the source of soulfulness is.[97]

Upon the peak of bliss humanity should chime along with the heavenly spirits' song of praise. These spirits constantly glorify God with their burning devotion. When humanity joins in they should bring to fulfillment that which the fallen angel has ruined through his arrogance. The human is therefore the sterling "tenth one"

---

97. PL 197, 747C.

(tenth chorus) who completes all of this through God's power.[98]

[God said:] "I gave the splendour which the first angel yielded to humans—to Adam and his race."[99]

Matthew: It would seem that Hildegard's understanding of humanity is that of splendor. That word, splendor, is a word that includes *doxa*, glory, radiance, light-images that Hildegard has been using to convey the beauty and glory of the angels.

Hildegard is actually saying that God has taken the splendor that Lucifer and his followers left behind when they plunged into darkness and handed it on to humanity, which is a sign of our deep beauty but also of our responsibility, implying that we ought to do a better job than they. Interestingly and surprisingly—I've not found this in any other writer—she adds us as the tenth chorus. Nine choruses of angels exist and then we human beings constitute a tenth chorus. In several places she talks about ten as the golden number. So she certainly has a very exalted understanding of the power, grace, and beauty of the human being. She says we receive "the place and the honour of the lost angels."

She talks about turning toward the east, "the origin of holy transformation." East represents the rising of the sun, the new-day creativity. Again, psychology and cosmology are connected. Like many native peoples, Hildegard does not separate the human psyche from the cosmos. The expansiveness of one parallels the expansiveness of the other. One is inside the other. Instead of a psychology of an introspective consciousness, she presents a psychology of microcosm-macrocosm.

When she says that we pick up the splendor and power and light of the bad angels who have fallen on earth, this implies that we can

98. *Scivias* 11, 2,
99. *Scivias* 111, 1.

do what they did with it. Or we can make different choices. She's emphasizing our moral responsibility.

Human Community With The Angels

God breathed into humans a spirit of life: and so living humans became flesh and blood. Thereupon God gave humans the society of the angels with their praise and their services.[100]

God created the human with body and soul. Within the body God included all corporal nature and within the soul God included an image of the angelic spirit.[101]

Matthew: Hildegard celebrates the creation of the human being as not only including a relationship to all living things through flesh and blood on earth, but also as part of the community of the angels. In addition, she says that God drew all creatures in human beings; in other words, the human being is a microcosm of the macrocosm, and we are interdependent with all the other creatures. We need them. And yet, according to Hildegard, we're not just related to the visible creatures but to the invisible ones, to the angelic spirits. Our soul, she believes, is an image of that angelic spirit.

All this certainly emphasizes Hildegard's appreciation of the unique power, radiance, and responsibility of the human being.

Rupert: All creation, according to the traditional view, is mediated and governed through the angels. But the idea that we share the society of the angels implies conscious connections and interactions with them.

Of course, Hildegard was thinking in terms of the biblical story of creation. But if we look at this in the context of evolution, one of the great and mysterious steps in the evolutionary process is the appearance

---

100. PL 197, 272D.
101. PL 197, 945C.

of human consciousness. We haven't a clue when it happened or how it happened. Nor for that matter do we have much clue what it is, in spite of all the neurophysiology that's been done in recent decades.

From the fossil record we see a series of human or near-human skeletons and skulls stretching back a million years, two million years. We keep finding even older ones. But did these people talk? We don't know. Some people think language only came about some fifty thousand years ago. Others think it is much more ancient. What were our remote ancestors doing, what were they thinking, what were they up to? We haven't a clue.

But something obviously happened, a creative leap. And that leap is understood in traditional societies in terms of the communion of human beings with spirits. Traditional hunter-gatherer societies all have a belief that people, and especially shamans, can commune with ancestors, with animal spirits, and a variety of other spirits, some of which are flying spirits. We find these traditions all around the world.

Could it be that the creative jump in human consciousness happened when there was in fact a conscious contact between human beings and nonhuman spirits? Perhaps there actually was a meeting of human beings and the realm of the angels. Maybe this society with angels is precisely what led to the evolution of human consciousness as we know it.

Every tradition has creation myths in which the origin of various human activities—the use of fire, tools, song, dance, language, culture—are initiated by gods, heroes, or spirit beings. All myths speak of an eruption of creative power from another dimension, from a realm of spirits. Some people today interpret these myths in an extraordinarily literal sense in terms of extraterrestrials coming to guide us, whether in UFOs or whatever. But the role of superhuman beings is so universal in myths that it suggests to me that there really was, in the evolution of human consciousness, a series of creative jumps that involved contacts with angelic intelligences.

My friend Terence McKenna was very keen on the role of psychedelics in shamanism. He believed that in many psychedelic experiences there is a meeting with spirits, with nonhuman minds, and one of the things they do is communicate information. In his book *The Food of the Gods* he argues that the opening up of consciousness through psychedelic experience, and in those realms making contact with other conscious entities, is a key to understanding the origins and evolution of human consciousness.

Not everyone would like to follow him all the way in his emphasis on the central role of psychedelics, though there's no doubt that they are used in many cultures. But visionary states can also arise in many other ways.

I think this passage in Hildegard has something very relevant to say to us today. To my mind, this connection between human beings and angels is as good a hypothesis as any, and better than most.

Matthew: The word society that you pointed to also implies some kind of equality. In Hildegard's teaching about human beings and angels, there is some kind of shared communication and equality. If this happened in the past, as you point out, through leaps of consciousness, language, culture, and art, why can't it happen now as well? A society that is inclusive of these spirits is more needed now than ever before.

As for psychedelic experiences, I would just propose that, as you say, many other ways exist to lead us to visionary states. Ways such as fasting and chanting and meditation and sweat lodges and dancing and worship (at least worship ought to lead to visionary states)—all these should be available to all our people.

Rupert: Another implication of Hildegard's teaching is that human beings are unique among creatures on earth because of their conscious communion with the angels. Hence they have a special role to play as intermediaries between the spirit realm and the biological and terrestrial realms.

Angels Are Amazed By Us

All of the angels are amazed at humans, who through their holy works appear clothed with an incredibly beautiful garment.[102]

For the angel without the work of the flesh is simply praise; but the humans with their corporeal works are a glorification: therefore the angels praise humans' work.[103]

Matthew: I find these passages to be among the most stunning in all of Hildegard's angelology. When most people think of angels, if they think of them at all, they are amazed at angels and feel inferior to the angels.

But here we have Hildegard saying the angels are amazed at us. What dignity and healthy pride that gives our species! And why are they amazed at us? Because of our holy works. Angels only choose once. But we, with our constant creativity, entering so fully into the evolutionary habits of the universe, are unfolding and yet doing so often consciously and deliberately, by choice. I hear Hildegard saying that our works, our choices, astound the angels. It's wonderful.

And then she says the angel is simply praise, but the human being is a glorification. That is one more reason why the angels praise humanity's works. Again she's honoring matter here, she's honoring flesh. In one way she's saying that the angels' life compared with ours is much duller. It's simply praise, it's predictable, whereas ours is constantly bringing new things into the world and even praise out of the angels.

We are an unusual species. So often we see the shadow side of our being. We are a bridge between the material world and the spirit world, and it gets us down. How badly we fail both worlds! But here Hildegard extols this unique experiment on God's part, our being both spirit and body.

---

102. PL 197, 865D.
103. PL 197, 1061C.

She's saying that we are fascinating, we are amazing, we are praiseworthy to the angels. I think this needs deep meditation. It would help us to get our dignity back. When we do that, we'll start acting better.

Angels Praise The Good Works Of Humanity

The angels lift up their voices to God in praise of the good works of humanity. They continually praise the ever-increasing good works of humankind. They climb onto the golden altar which stands before God's countenance. And from now on they intone a new song to honour these works.[104]

Matthew: I think Hildegard means that humanity represents a new song to the universe, a new song to these vibratory and deeply musical beings, the angels. We have inspired them to intone a new song simply to welcome us, to honor our works.

Rupert: This implies that by singing this new song, we change the celestial consciousness. The consciousness of God and of the entire universe is changed by human evolution. We normally think of human evolution as being an entirely provincial event here on Earth. Humans can go as far as the moon, rockets can reach Mars and Venus and other planets, but we don't go beyond the solar system. There's nothing we've ever done that physically goes beyond, except maybe very weak radio waves. The influence of human works, in the modern cosmological context, is very limited.

But Hildegard gives a very different perspective. "All of the angels are amazed at humans" (page 160). Their new song, inspired by human works, is sung to God. This implies a cosmic effect of humanity. What human beings do on Earth makes a difference to the conscious spirits of the entire universe, which is a very big thought indeed.

---

104. PL 197, 236C.

Matthew: And it's a very optimistic and hopeful thought. A pride-bearing thought. It's very expansive. As Aquinas says, "When your mind expands, joy comes." Empowerment goes with it. A lot of the disempowerment that our culture has felt in the last hundred years might be washed out, purified, cleaned up, by such news as this. If human beings knew that beautiful, good, and powerful beings were watching us, maybe we would stand up more erect and be more beautiful ourselves. We would be inspired to live up to our dignity.

The Language Of The Angels

The omnipotent God spoke to Adam in the words of the angels, because Adam knew their language well and could understand it. Through the reason which God had given him and through the spirit of the prophets' talents, Adam possessed the knowledge of all the languages which would later be invented by humans.[105]

Rupert: This passage says that the communication between God and Adam was through angelic language. Adam, before the Fall, was in full communion with this realm of angels, a communion interrupted by the Fall.

Not only did the first human being connect with the angelic spirits and understand their mode of communication, but this played a key role in the origin of human language. Adam spoke the prototype of all human languages, the primal language that evolved into all the later languages. According to Genesis, Adam was invited by God to name all the living creatures, and he did so. The first human language arose in full awareness of the language of the angels, and also in full awareness of how it implied all subsequent human languages.

---

105. PL 197, 1041C.

From a scientific point of view, no one knows how language arose or evolved. It's one of the great mysteries. You can't dig up fossil languages. All you dig up are solid, durable things like flint arrowheads and bones. We don't know anything about the sounds that people made when the first languages evolved. Nor do we know whether human languages all arose from a single creative event or whether there were several independent origins of languages.

Some linguists, like Noam Chomsky, believe that all human languages participate in a common archetypal grammar, a universal grammar. There is a common basis of all human language, which would imply a common origin for all languages.

Hildegard raises all these questions in this brief remark, and they're still big questions for us today.

Matthew: When I hear you speak about the naming of the animals that is referred to in the biblical creation story, I think of the recent discoveries of the caves in southern France. People from twenty-five thousand years ago were naming, in pictures, horses, antelope, lions. Naming is something to do with classification, or seeing families. And that ability to see and thereby name kinship groups seems a special power of our species. Of course, we distort it when we get too tribal or clannish ourselves. But it's a spiritual breakthrough, it seems to me, to be able to honor both the diversity and the sameness in things.

When we speak of language, it seems to me that would include painting and carving and image making. It brings in what Jung called the collective unconscious and archetypes, common symbols and metaphors that go way, way back. Which may help to explain why in spiritual traditions so many metaphors are essentially the same. The metaphors of light, fire, and darkness seem to imply a common language and a common experience, a profound experience shared.

Human Language

The angels, who are spirits, cannot speak in a comprehensible language. Language is therefore a particular mission for humanity.[106]

Matthew: I think Hildegard is distinguishing between the communication that a vibratory, pure spirit expresses and our experience of language here on earth. She is praising our capacity for comprehensible language, which she calls a particular mission for humanity. Once again she's underscoring the implications of our being spirit and matter. In language we are bringing together the power of both. Any animals on earth can express themselves and communicate, but she's implying there's a richness to the human capacity, and also a holy responsibility to honor the word and render it genuinely truthful and comprehensible.

She's setting us off from angels. The angels may have alerted us, opened us up to the level of consciousness that includes language, but only the human being could carry it from there. Angels are spirits, and their language is thus more universal than ours.

Rupert: It may be more universal than ours in the sense that they sing. But it may be less concerned with communication than ours is. Comprehensible language is the basis of human culture. And human culture is evolutionary. Probably angels aren't into culture in the same way that we are, but are primarily occupied with praise and harmony. This gives another reason for angels to be amazed at what human beings do.

Guardian Angels

Because God has determined that the angels would give assistance to humans in the area of protection, God also made them part of the human community.[107]

---

106. PL 197, 1045A.
107. Hildegard of Bingen, *Causae et Curae* (Leipzig: P Kaiser, 1903), 26, 53.

From the almighty God manifold, mighty, and divinely majestic illuminating powers come. These powers come in order to be helpful and supportive to those who truly fear God and those who loyally love in their poverty of spirit, and to encompass these people with the soft glow of their work.[108]

Rupert: Hildegard has talked about angels praising God and human beings entering into the community of praise with the angels. Now she talks about the guardian role of angels: protecting people and supporting them. But she implies that this support is conditional. They help those who fear God and who are open to the divine spirit. But they don't seem so able or willing to protect people who are not open to God's love.

Matthew: Yes. This brings out again the relationship between the human being and spirits—it's give and take—and human beings aren't here just to take. Maybe that's why Hildegard says that in protecting us, God makes them part of the human community; and community includes the dimension of equality, give-and-take in relationship. It also helps to explain why some people seem to live lives that are anything but touched by the angels.

Rupert: They may be touched by the bad angels. There's the long Jewish, Christian, and Islamic tradition of each of us having two personal angels: one good, one bad. Guardian angels have their shadows. Those people who don't open themselves to the spirit of God and the help of the guardian angel are likely to be influenced by the dark angel. Rather than being immune from angelic influence, they are influenced by the wrong kind.

Matthew: In league with fallen powers and principalities. But I'm struck by the fact that while it's in Jewish and Muslim lore that we have a guardian angel on one side of us and a demonic angel on the other, as far as I can see this is not in Hildegard.

---

108. *Scivias* 1, 1.

Angels Help Those Who Call On God

If a human only sighs the name of its parent, God, then God calls the human back into proper behaviour and the protection of the angels rushes to the human's side so that they will no longer be harmed by their enemy.[109]

Matthew: Hildegard seems to be saying that if we simply call on God, the angels rush in to protect us. But if the angels have to rush in, this implies that they're not exactly sitting on our shoulder in the first place. But maybe that's a minute point. It is our prayer and our calling on God that invites the angels into our sphere of concern, and thereby they play out their role as guardians, as protectors.

Rupert: It's interesting that here Hildegard is talking of angels in the plural, rather than simply an individual guardian angel, which she doesn't directly mention.

It's not clear to me what kind of protection these angels are giving. When she says "they will no longer be harmed by their enemy," does this mean enemy in the sense of the evil angels, or moral danger, or does it refer to harm from a physical enemy? For example, if they're in a fight, will the angels rush in to protect them from a human enemy?

Matthew: She says, "God calls the human back into proper behaviour." This implies that she's talking especially of the onslaught of moral enemies.

Conscience

One's good conscience points to the angelic powers of battle which praise and serve God. But the bad conscience reveals God's power. For it attacks God, and this drove the first persons out of Paradise. This is the general situation of decision for all

---

109. PL 197, 898B.

humans. Those who decide things and act with a good conscience show thereby God's goodness. But those who act according to a bad conscience thereby prove God's power.[110]

Rupert: The distinction here is between good conscience and bad conscience, and the bad conscience is presumably under the influence of the fallen angels. Conscience is not simply an aspect of individual consciousness, but is open to angelic powers, good and evil, that come to influence it. Our conscience is a battleground, part of the larger battleground between the good and evil angels.

Matthew: Yes. I see her zeroing in on the decision-making process, which has also everything to do with our creativity. We can use our creativity in league with the good angels or in league with the demonic spirits.

Aquinas understands conscience as essentially the decisions we make, linked to the dimension of reason. During the modern era, the stress on individualism has meant that for many people conscience has become some kind of ghost in the machine whispering in our ear what is right. In other words, conscience is located exclusively in the realm of the subjective. But today we as a species are facing many conscience issues: eating habits; our relationships to future generations and to the soil, the forests, the waters; the relationship of northern and southern peoples, rich and poor. These are anything but individual or subjective. They have to do with the survival of the community and society and earth as we know it. Our understanding of conscience has to reclaim this dimension of decision-making around the common good. And society, in Hildegard's view, includes the angelic powers. Our decisions are not just private or personal, but they have to do with the cosmic struggle of good and evil.

Rupert: Hildegard's discussion of guardian angels is mainly concerned with the moral dimension, and doesn't seem to bear much relation to all these contemporary stories of angels who help people

---

110. PL 197, 898D.

in emergencies, often manifesting in human bodies, offering practical help at moments of danger.

Matthew: I agree. Many people in our time seem to be experiencing angels at the level of self-protection. Hildegard is more interested in the moral arena of protection. Might this reflect a certain narcissism on the part of our culture, where we think the worst thing is dying or physical injury? The tradition is saying the worst thing is moral death and spiritual corruption. Hildegard is challenging us to think again more in terms of society, its need for moral sustenance, courage, and wisdom. These are the real issues of survival that angels care most passionately about, more than just the survival of the individual.

Rupert: Perhaps the angelic manifestations reported in so many recent books about angels, although concerned in many cases with physical survival, could possibly represent a way in which the angels are helping morally too. These acts of physical help may, and I think in many cases do, awaken people to the existence of another dimension, a hidden dimension of life.

Hildegard did not live in a secular society dominated by atheistic and secular philosophies. She lived in an age of great faith, when people were building great cathedrals all over Europe. The invisible power of God, the angels, and the saints were part of the consensus reality. Not everyone was open to the spiritual realm, but its existence was not in question.

Today the very existence of a spiritual dimension is in question. Maybe in our age angels can help through practical, physical manifestations to awaken us to the reality of superhuman intelligences.

Humans Cannot See Angels In Their True Form

The three angels who appeared to Abraham as he sat at the entrance to his tent showed themselves in human form because in no way can humans see angels in their true form. Because of their altering forms, humans are unable to see an unalterable spirit.[111]

Matthew: Hildegard puts it very strongly—"In no way can humans see angels in their true form." All of these wonderful paintings we have of angels, at the Annunciation, for example, or at the birth of Christ, make you wonder what form these angels took.

The experiences I've had in praying with indigenous peoples are of spirits who come as light or as wind or as sound. Hildegard is not saying angels have to come in human form, they just don't come in their totally true form. We can't experience them that way. I guess it's about leaving one's mind open.

Rupert: There are parallels with the UFO literature. There are persistent reports of UFOs and alien visitors, which tend to be experienced in the imagery of science fiction. It's possible that some of these are angelic manifestations of one kind or another. It may be that angels feel that by manifesting as UFOs they'll get through to some people better than in any other form. But the official view within science, within the political establishment, and within the church is to dismiss or explain away these reports. I must admit, I share this prejudice against UFOs and aliens.

Matthew: In America today there are more young people who believe in the reality of UFOs than believe that the social security system will be intact when they reach retirement age. Maybe angels have taken to the skyways in spaceships, as you say, to get more attention. Like Greenpeace took to rubber dinghies to get attention. It's hard getting contemporary people's attention if you're an angel.

Like you, I'm a little uneasy. And I think that a good deal of the answers would be found if our military establishments were less secretive than they are. I met a fellow recently who sat me down and went through a theory on how he thinks the military contacted

---

111. PL 197, 1043A.

extraterrestrials years ago, and they've been getting clues on how to build these spaceships, and they've been putting them together, housing them in the mountains of Utah or something. I was quite taken aback, because this fellow didn't seem particularly far-out until he came to that part of his conversation.

Rupert: There's no doubt that traditional ideas about good and bad angels fighting each other, and an apocalyptic war in heaven, are taken up in science fiction. *Star Wars*, for instance.

These are deep archetypes. In the modern world they're played out mainly in the arena of science fiction, and when people have experiences of otherness, those experiences are often dressed in this science fiction garb. And I think that this is part of the UFO phenomenon. They didn't have science fiction in the Middle Ages, but rather a well-developed angelology.

With the decline of general belief in angels and the secularization of the cosmos, these archetypes are still widely recognized, but reinterpreted in science fiction terms: flying around in spaceships rather than with wings.

Matthew: Mechanized.

Rupert: Yes, they've been mechanized. Our image of the cosmos was mechanized, and the angels got mechanized too. And instead of angels moving at the speed of thought, as Hildegard expressed it, now science fiction has conventions like time warps that enable them to do much the same thing.

Matthew: Maybe this too, more positively speaking, is a striving to develop the imagination. Now that our universe has suddenly taken tremendous leaps in terms of size, mystery, complexity, and history, we're groping for a language, an art form, images by which to understand our relationship in the universe. One thing about UFO stories is they're about relationships, even if it's a kidnapping. Even if it's the Pentagon getting secrets from Martian maneuvers, it's about a relationship.

You were talking about archetypes. I think an ultimate archetype is how we're related to the rest of the universe. Is it benign? Who are these invisible forces? And that is what the whole discussion on angels is about.

Our imaginations are being challenged. Our artists, our storytellers are being challenged to assist us in naming the nature of the community to which we really belong. And maybe UFOs are just the first stumbling effort.

Rupert: Or maybe a stopgap measure until we can recover a sense of these broader dimensions that the ancient tradition of angels, of spirits found in all traditions, can give us. As we recover a new sense of the life of nature, maybe we can go beyond these rather crudely mechanical metaphors into a much enlarged realm of imagination.

Matthew: The UFO may prove to be the last machine invented by the modern era. The next step is, as you say, angels. The reconnecting of our imaginations to the spiritual tradition.

How Angels Take On Human Forms

According to their nature angels are invisible but they take their bodies from the atmosphere and appear visible in the human form to those they are sent to as messengers. They also adopt other human habits. They do not speak to humans with angelic tongues, but instead with words that can be understood. They eat as humans do, but their food evaporates like dew which continually sinks on to the grass and is instantaneously drunk up in the sun's glow. The evil spirits can also adopt the form of any creature in order to seduce humans.[112]

---

112. PL 197, 1043C.

Rupert: Here Hildegard is talking about the shape-shifting powers of angels, who can manifest in almost any form appropriate to the circumstances. They can speak in human tongues if necessary, and can appear to be human even to the extent of eating, which is often taken as a criterion for separating a spirit from a proper embodied being. Their embodiment can have a curiously real and literal presence. She even considers the physiology of angelic digestion. I like the way she deals with the question of what happens to the food when the angel eats it. It simply evaporates like the dew!

She also says that evil spirits can adopt the form of any creature in order to seduce human beings. Both angels and devils are able to take on any form in order to communicate or relate to human beings. But since these forms are only manifestations, they're presumably in most cases short-lived.

Matthew: Yet I hope she's not opening the Pandora's box of the witch-hunts, pogroms, and so forth. Spirits taking over human bodies, cats, familiars, and the like. That to me would be a very scary corollary of that sentence.

Rupert: She's not talking about possession, but manifestation. She said they can take the form of any creature. She's not here dealing with the question of demonic possession, but rather of angels and devils taking human or other forms, and even appearing to eat. But I agree with you that there's plenty of scope for paranoia here.

Matthew: Now we know why the machine universe took over.

Rupert: It's a much more hygienic and straightforward place.

Matthew: And a much more boring place.

Rupert: A machine universe purged of evil spirits must have been an enormous relief in the seventeenth century, against the background of witch-hunts all over Europe, and in New England too. But it also involved stripping the universe of the angelic orders.

Matthew: It was a sterile place, much like a contemporary hospital. It was necessary because of what I call right-brain excess.

Rupert: Yes. It's a universe sterilized against spirits. I think the other side of any spiritual faith is a recognition of the demonic. Any religious or spiritual path that recognizes the existence of good spirits at the same time recognizes the existence of bad ones.

Therefore if we have a revival of spirituality, we'll also have a revival of belief in the power of evil spirits. I think it's an inevitable corollary of spiritual faith and of a spiritual worldview. This is one reason that secular humanists and rationalists are so against any form of religion. If you allow good angels back, you'll get bad angels back too, together with spells and superstition, the nightmare vision of witchcraft that the mechanistic, rationalistic view of the world was supposed to have expelled forever.

These texts of Hildegard, like those of Dionysius and Aquinas and the Bible itself, make it quite clear that fallen angels are part of the deal. You can't have good angels without bad ones. There's no cozy, New Age vision on offer here, with good angels that are always filled with soft, gentle vibrations, like New Age music in a universe from which all evil forces have been comfortably expelled.

Matthew: So you can't just insert the good angel into a sterile, mechanized, hygienic world; you've got to bring the shadow ones back too.

Rupert: That's what this tradition tells us.

Matthew: I think it is appropriate to name the evil spirits of our time with our own names, such as: Racism, Sexism, Colonialism, Anthropocentrism, Injustice, and so forth. These are the "Beelzebubs" of our civilization.

Jesus And The Angels

When God's son was born from his Mother upon earth, he appeared in heaven in the Father so that the angels trembled forthwith and exultingly intoned honey-flowing songs of praise. At this the heavenly kettle-drums and zithers and all kinds of musical sounds sounded out in indescribable harmony and beauty; for humanity which had lain in corruption was raised into bliss. But the Father presented the resurrected son with unveiled wounds to the heavenly choruses: "This is my beloved son!" At this an immeasurable joy was awoken in the angels. This joy surpasses all human comprehension. For with this the evil past, in which God was not recognised, was wrestled down. Human reason, which had been suppressed through the devil's influence, is lifted up to recognition of God. Through the highest blessing the path of truth is revealed to humans, and they are guided back from death into life.[113]

Matthew: Here Hildegard is celebrating the renewed relationship between humanity and God and the angels. That is what the Incarnation is about. The coming of God in the person of Jesus has deep implications for angelology for Hildegard. It awakens the angels. She says they "trembled ... and exultingly intoned honey-flowing songs of praise." She pictures the angels as rolling out the kettledrums and zithers and becoming very musical again about the joy that this possibility brings to their work.

Rupert: What do you think she means when she says, "He appeared in heaven in the Father"?

Matthew: It's probably a reference to the Logos being reflected in a new way in the Father now that the son is born of a mother on earth. It's a new dimension to the fatherhood of God. It's the Cosmic Christ spanning the entire universe.

Rupert: That implies a change within the Holy Trinity as well as a change within the angelic orders. It therefore implies evolution not just in the angelic realms but also in the divine nature.

---

113. *Scivias* 11, I.

Matthew: Sure. Eckhart is explicit on that. He says, "God becomes as creatures express God."[114] And how else could it be? As evolution happens, as nature unfolds, including human nature that now encompasses the Logos, divinity would be affected.

Deep within the heart of Christian Trinitarian belief is an affirmation of the vulnerability of God. And this is very Jewish. It was a Hellenistic notion that God is the unmoved mover, the stable point in the sky. But this is not Jewish. Rabbi Heschel talks about divinity being really dependent on human evolution, human activity of justice, and compassion.

We have to wrestle our doctrines away from a static cosmology in which they become encrusted. In such a context they easily lose their energy, become rusty. In the context of a new cosmology, all these doctrines take on a tremendous life and energy. Our best mystics, like Eckhart and Hildegard, had deep intuitions of this, of divinity unfolding as the universe unfolds. And certainly the Christ story is part of that unfolding.

Rupert: This also agrees then with the earlier remarks of Hildegard about the angels being amazed at human works (pages 160-161). The angels are responding and reacting to what happens on earth. They have to, if they're in interaction with the course of events in the cosmos and with the development of humanity. But, as you say, Hildegard is going further in implying an actual change in the divine nature. She is getting away from this Greek notion of changeless, Platonic forms beyond space and time, totally immutable and impassive.

Matthew: And part of the angels' excitement and admiration is to see the story of Jesus unfold. Within the tradition, angels are present at all the critical moments in Jesus' life: at the Annunciation,

---

114. See Matthew Fox, *Breakthrough: Meister Eckhart's Creation Spirituality in New Translation* (New York: Doubleday, 1980), 77.

his conception; at his birth; in his experience of baptism; in his going into the desert where he was succored by angels as he wrestled with the demons and was tempted by Satan in the garden of Gethsemane and at the Resurrection and the Ascension. It's not as if the angels were just spectators, any more than they are with us. They're real participants in the unfolding story of the Cosmic Christ in Jesus. The cosmic forces, however you name them, are participants in the life-story of any being, certainly any human being.

God Became A Human Being, Not An Angel

Oh how great is the joy that God became human. Among the angels God exists as divinity, but among humans God exists as a human![115]

Matthew: Hildegard here is exultant in the realization that in relationship with divinity, human beings have more going for them than the angels. God is still God among the angels. God did not become an angel but did become a human being. This moves her to exult in the joy of being human. She sees the Incarnation as a tremendous affirmation of esteem for the human species.

Rupert: In some pictures, Christ is shown as the king of the angels. Was that a common understanding?

Matthew: Absolutely. In all the Cosmic Christ hymns from the early church, Christ is portrayed as having power over the angels. This is to show that there's nothing to fear from the invisible forces of the universe; they are being used for benign purposes by the Christ.

Rupert: Presumably the idea of the Blessed Virgin Mary as Queen of the Angels is a further development of the same theme. Or

---

115. PL 197, 946B.

is it a reversion to a much earlier archetype of the goddess as Queen of Heaven, as the maternal aspect of space and of the cosmos?

Matthew: I think it's all those things together. Mary, Queen of the Angels, is again a tremendous affirmation of humanity's beauty: one of us, in addition to the Christ, is overseeing the role of angels in the heavens, and that is the feminine principle, the goddess. Indeed, Hildegard paints Mary as the conductress of the symphonies of the celestial spheres in heaven—she directs the music there among human beings and angels alike.

Angels Are Present At Human Deaths

[When it comes to the point of death] the good and bad angels are present, the witnesses of all the deeds which the person has completed in and with her body. They await the end in order to bring the person with them after the dissolution.[116]

Matthew: There exists an ancient tradition that the angels are present at the time of death. Today, interest in this tradition has been renewed by people reporting their near-death experiences. The angels are not just present for the expression of being called our lifetime. They were present before our existence, and await its further expressions. The promise is that they await the end in order to take the person with them to another realm,

Rupert: Does "dissolution" mean dissolution of the body?

Matthew: I think so.

Rupert: The idea of winged beings as soul guides or psychopomps is very ancient. The Egyptians had a similar idea, and there are Egyptian pictures of winged soul guides over mummies. The Greeks too had the idea of soul guides taking the soul through the heavenly spheres. The

---

116. *Scivias* 1, 4.

same idea is expressed in Victorian cemeteries, with statues of angels over the graves.

Although we hear a lot in modern near-death accounts of the beings of light at the time of death, we don't hear so much about the bad angels. Presumably the bad angels are not merely there to watch the good angels lead souls onward and upward. They must have a role to play. What is it?

Matthew: I suspect our entrance into death is not unlike our entrance into other creative moments of our lives. The bad angels and the good angels are there for our decision-making, and even at death there are decisions to be made. For example, the choice of despair, bitterness, recrimination, and regret. I think all those could be symbolized by the presence of bad angels tempting us. Whereas the good angels would encourage us to respond with what was hopefully a pattern of our lives—generosity, trust, and surrender, which characterize a holy death as much as a holy life. I see this as an affirmation that death is a creative act on the part of the human being; in some ways, it is a moral act. We have a decision as to how to approach it. Therefore, the angels both bad and good are present.

Rupert: I'm curious to know what happens to those who are taken off by the bad angels. How do you envisage it?

Matthew: You'd better talk to Dante about that. But this also connects to another teaching of Hildegard about the Last Judgment. I get the impression that she's writing about our creative decisions in this lifetime: every creative act is a last judgment because you don't get to redo it. It's a one and only choice. She melts down the dualism between this life and the next, and between heaven and hell and earth. She is saying, in effect, that our choices bring about hell on earth or heaven on earth.

Angels At The Eucharist

When the priest, dressed with the holy vestments, stepped to the altar for the celebration of the divine mysteries, a bright splendour of light suddenly fell from the heavens. Angels stepped down, and light flooded around the altar. It remained this way until after the completion of the holy offering when the priest withdrew. After the Gospel of peace was read out and the offerings were laid upon the altar for consecration, the priest sang the praise of the omnipotent God: "Holy, holy, holy, Lord God Sabaoth!" and he began that unpronounceable mystery. At this moment the heavens opened up. A fiery flash of indescribably bright clarity fell down upon the offerings and streamed through them with its majesty, just as the sun penetrates with its light when it streams upon an object. … Angels climb down and light floods the altar. … Heavenly spirits bow towards holy service.[117]

Matthew: In this passage from her first book, *Scivias*, Hildegard is describing a spiritual experience she had during mass. In doing so, she is invoking an ancient tradition that part of the angels' work is to be present for worship. This is deeply embedded in the Jewish tradition. And indeed this passage in the Western liturgy that Hildegard invokes is Jewish in origin and concerns the angels: "Holy, holy, holy, Lord God of Hosts, heaven and Earth are filled with your glory, hosanna in the highest."

Right at the high point of the Western liturgy there is this invocation of the angels. Hildegard does not present this as theology or theory but talks about her own experience. It was a very powerful experience for her, and it is an experience that people yearn for today. If praise is an important part of the angels' work, it is also an important part of humanity's spiritual life. As Rabbi Heschel says, "Praise precedes faith." We need these breakthroughs that take faith beyond intelligence into experience. And what better place than where the community gathers to praise and invoke all the beings of the universe, including the angels?

---

117. *Scivias* 11, 6.

Native people teach that the center of the universe is the center of a praying circle. This was Jewish teaching too—the temple was the center of the universe. Today we are redefining the center of the universe not as a single place but as many places where energy is high. We need to discover how worship is a centering place for the universe. Hildegard teaches this too. She says the altar is the center of the universe. Angels would be there, since they like to be where the divine action is.

Healthy worship opens up the channels of communication between angel and human being in the presence of praising and honoring the Godhead. We have to re-create forms of worship that allow the angels access again, and allow human beings to open the heart up so praise can happen. We need to move beyond the head to all the chakras, so that all the energies of the universe can be present, microcosm with macrocosm.

Rupert: I agree it's very interesting that she speaks here not from a theoretical but from an experiential point of view. I would be very interested in an empirical survey of people who go to services to find out in which moments they have been moved deeply. I've had moments in church services when I've felt a great sense of divine or angelic presence. I imagine many people have had such experiences, but nowadays people are very shy in talking about them, as they are shy in talking about mystical experiences in general.

Matthew: Sure. Our mystical experiences have been relegated to the "subjective" realm by our modern mentality. A kind of private-property notion prevails about them, encompassing them in secrecy like our bank accounts are held in secret.

Hildegard seems to have had experiences like this, with angels climbing down and lights flooding the altar, without going to an outside source. The fact that many people today are seeking outside sources such as psychedelics is a statement about how forms of worship are not fulfilling their function. If religion is to renew itself, to do its primary work, which is to awaken the mind and heart to our place in the universe and communion with other beings, we need forms of worship that make such experiences possible.

Make Friends With Good Angels

Say I, Christ, to you children of humans: Make yourselves friends with both the good angels and with human injustice and truthfulness. Because of this justice and truthfulness the angels will enjoy your good deeds and will one day take you up to the eternal dwelling-place.[118]

Matthew: Hildegard often breaks into the first person of God or Christ, and speaks as if she's been taken over by their voice. These are instances for Hildegard of particular importance and moment. And here she is Christ telling us to make friends with good angels. This is an appropriate way to complete our investigation of Hildegard's teaching on angels, the final word being that we befriend angels when we befriend justice and truthfulness in our own lives.

The mechanistic or modern worldview was not friendly to mystics or angels. But Hildegard, working out of a premodern worldview, calls us in our postmodern times to pay more attention to these relationships, and she points out that it is the spiritual experience of truth and justice that leads us into communion with the angels, and therefore into friendship. The justice dimension corresponds, of course, to Aquinas's teaching of the relationship between angels and prophets.

Rupert: But do you think there are practical ways of making friends with the angels? For example, in various Jewish ceremonies there are invocations of the archangels Michael, Uriel, Raphael, and Gabriel as the guardians of the four directions. And Christians in the

---

118. *Liber Vitae Meritorum*, 320.

Catholic tradition have a particular opportunity to make friends with the angels at Michaelmas, the feast of St. Michael and All Angels, on 29 September. Do you think there are things we can do apart from being more open to God, and the spirit of truth and justice, specifically to invoke the angels?

Matthew: Yes, there are rituals and invocations that are present already in church traditions, and some that have to be resurrected. And we need new rituals to invoke the angels; I think that these will come as we allow our minds to wander more into the living cosmos. Technology could play a great role in helping us envision the angels—for example, the wonderful photographs we now have of stars being born and galaxies spiraling. But I don't think we should underestimate the path of the struggle for justice and truthfulness. This is about inner work. Certainly truthfulness is. Hildegard is saying that where there is this inner work, it does indeed open the communication with angels.

The same is true in struggling for justice. Remember that angels often visit people in prison. St. Peter was liberated from prison by an angel. Sometimes I think that Gandhi and Martin Luther King, Jr., and other great souls that have spent time in prison have found angelic support there.

So the struggle for justice is not an abstraction. It's a way of learning and a way of opening the heart. I know one Catholic sister, for example, a very fine and holy woman, who tells me her greatest mystical experience is being taken away in the paddy wagon by police when she protests at military bases and nuclear power plants—that is when she most feels the presence of spirits and the angels.

So the struggle for justice is a path that opens our hearts up and allows angels to rush in. This struggle, certainly around ecological issues, is going to get more intense in our lifetime, and we need to see these struggles as rituals. And angels come to healthy and authentic rituals.

Rupert: That's an exciting prospect, the struggle for justice and the struggle for a new relationship with the environment taking place in alliance with the angels and with their help. It gives it a bigger dimension. It is an empowering thought, because otherwise it's just a handful of people fighting against huge vested interests and economic and political powers. We need all the help we can get.

Matthew: And surely then guardian angels of children must be awfully interested in the ecological crisis. The children's future depends on a healthy planet.

CONCLUSION

★ ★ ★

Angels in the Twenty-First Century

What is happening today is not merely a revival of interest in angels. The new cosmology raises new questions and greatly increases the scope for angelic action in the universe. We have today a great need to understand the role of consciousness beyond the human realms. These challenges require a revisioning of angelology, a new phase in our understanding of and relationship with the angelic realms.

We need to take stock of what we can learn from our tradition about angels. What do Dionysius the Areopagite, Hildegard of Bingen, and St. Thomas Aquinas have to teach us today about angels? Some of the lessons we have learned from these dialogues are:

- Angels are very numerous; they exist in astronomical numbers.
- There are many other kinds of consciousness in the cosmos besides human consciousness.
- Angels have been present from the origin of the universe.
- They exist in a hierarchic order of nested levels within levels.
- They are the governing intelligences of nature.
- They have a special relationship to light, fire, flames, and photons. There are astonishing parallels between Aquinas and

Einstein with regard to the nature of angels and of photons: in their locomotion and mode of movement, their agelessness, and their being massless.

- They are musical in nature and work in harmonious relationship with one another.
- The majority are friendly, but not all. Christ has power over the angels.
- They have a special relationship to human consciousness. We human beings help link the earthly world with cosmic intelligences.
- Angels may have played a special role in the birth of language.
- They inspire prophets and awaken human imagination and intuition, and thus befriend the artist in a special way.
- Angels are amazed at us, and our actions through the angels can affect the entire cosmos.
- Their primary role is praise.
- They have a variety of functions in their relationship with human beings, including inspiring, message-bearing, protecting, and guiding.
- They are present at holy worship.
- Both good and bad angels act in the arena of our conscience and decision making.
- They do not have material bodies but can temporarily assume the appearance of human or other bodies for the sake of communicating with and helping human beings.
- They accompany people from this life to the next.

QUESTIONS FOR THE FUTURE

At a time like ours it is not enough to call on the traditional teachings of religion and angelology. A new cosmology as well as a new Earth crisis demand more creative work on the part of those who inherit religious traditions. And so we conclude our discussion not with a statement of inherited wisdom, but with questions that come to us from the future about humanity's relation to the angels.

- How can we understand the consciousness of planets, stars, and galaxies?
- In the light of contemporary cosmology, can the traditional understanding of celestial intelligences help us interpret the self-organizing powers of planets, stars, and galaxies?
- Do angels have a role to play in the self-organizing dynamics of the microscopic world?
- In an evolutionary and expanding universe, are new species of angels coming into being as new forms, structures, and fields arise?
- What role do angels play in guiding the evolutionary process?
- Do angels evolve?
- How fast can angels communicate across the vastness of the universe?
- Do the fallen angels bring about evil in other conscious organisms residing in other parts of the universe?
- How can we befriend the good angels?
- Can the experience of and belief in angels, shared by all spiritual traditions, promote deep ecumenism?
- Can angels guide us through the social and ecological evils that surround us and threaten generations yet unborn?
- Can angels help us to revivify our forms of worship so that true praise might inspire prophetic vision and right action?
- Can our awakening to angels increase the capacity for communion?
- How can angels assist in resacralizing the work of artists?
- How can we, with the angels, resacralize the world?

APPENDIX

* * *

Angels in the Bible

The earlier writings of the Hebrew Bible are somewhat reticent about angelology. This owes no doubt to the fact that in developing a monotheism amid many peoples who were polytheistic, the Israelites were cautious about reintroducing old ways of thought about spirits and divine messengers. Only three angels—Gabriel, Michael, and Raphael—are mentioned by name in the Hebrew Bible, and the prophetic books rarely mention angels at all. In the later books, angels appear more frequently, especially in apocalyptic writings such as the Book of Daniel, where they play an important role. At this time monotheism was so well established in Jewish thinking that angels had no reason to be feared as objects of worship. At this time, too, other traditions such as the Zoroastrian religion of Persia influenced Israel with its emphasis on spirits.

In addition to the terms "angels" or "messengers," other titles of angels in the Hebrew scriptures include "sons of God," "the host of the Lord," "the host of heaven," and "the holy ones."

Angels abound in the Christian scriptures. This is especially the case with the infancy narratives of Jesus, with the ministry and mission of Christ, and with the apocalyptic literature such as the Book of Revelation. Angels represent the cosmic forces that come together in Jesus and that he employs for the good of the people. Paul mentions the nine choirs of angels or heavenly spirits, but his main emphasis is on how Christ holds power over the angels and all spiritual powers. Thus the temptation to be pessimistic about cosmic forces is done away with. The universe is essentially benign in all its aspects. Evil spirits cannot triumph over the power of the love of Christ.

In the Book of Revelation the angels play several roles, including praising at heavenly worship, ministering in the work of prophetic revelation, assisting in the governing of the world and the execution of the divine wishes, and guarding the seven churches of Asia, their leaders, and their communities.

Following is a list of biblical references to angels.

I. HEWBREW BIBLE

Genesis 16.7-11: The angel of Yahweh meets Hagar and instructs her to return to Sarai to bear a child (Ishmael). (Cf. 21.17.)

Genesis 19.1-26: Two angels whom Lot befriends with hospitality save him and his family from the destruction of Sodom.

Genesis 22.11-15: An angel intervenes to save Isaac from Abraham's knife.

Genesis 24.7, 40: Abraham promises his servant that an angel will lead him back to his homeland to choose a wife for Abraham's son, Isaac.

Genesis 28.12: Jacob dreams about angels of God going up and down a ladder to heaven.

Genesis 3 1. 11: An angel speaks to Jacob in a dream.

Genesis 32. 1: Angels meet Jacob on his journey and he calls the place of encounter "Mahanaim," saying, "this is God's camp."

Genesis 48.16: Manasseh blesses Joseph saying, "May the angel who has been my savior from all harm, bless these boys…"

Exodus 3.2: The angel of Yahweh appears to Moses in a burning bush.

Exodus 14.19: The angel of Yahweh marches at the front of the army of Israel.

Exodus 23.20-24: Yahweh promises an angel to protect the Israelites against their foes.

Exodus 32.34, 33.2: Yahweh promises to send an angel to go before the Israelites and protect them and fight their enemies.

Numbers 20.16: Moses sends a letter to the king of Edom saying that an angel brought the Israelites out of Egypt.

Numbers 22.22-35: The angel of Yahweh teaches Balaam to treat his donkey more kindly.

Deuteronomy 32.17: The Canticle of Moses rebukes those who "sacrificed to demons who are not God, to gods they did not know."

Judges 2.1, 4: The angel of Yahweh tells the Israelites that he has brought them from the land of Egypt.

Judges 5.23: In the Song of Deborah and Barak, Yahweh's angel curses Meroz.

Judges 6.11-24: An angel of Yahweh visits Gideon and tells him to deliver Israel.

Judges 13.3-25: An angel of Yahweh appears to Manoah's wife and informs her that she will give birth to a son; she names him Samson.

1 Samuel 29.9: David is said by Achish to be "as blameless as an angel."

2 Samuel 14.17, 20: David's wisdom is "like the angel of God," i.e., divine. (Cf. 2 Samuel 19.27.)

2 Samuel 24.16, 17: An angel carries out vengeance because of David's sins.

1 Kings 13.18: An angel tests whether a prophet will obey Yahweh.

1 Kings 19.5-7: An angel gets Elijah to strengthen himself through food for his journey.

2 Kings 1.3, 15: An angel tells Elijah to challenge Ahaziah, who sought help from the god of Ekron.

2 Kings 19.35: An angel of Yahweh decimates the Assyrian army, possibly by a plague.

1 Chronicles 2 1. 1: "Satan rose against Israel."

1 Chronicles 21.12-30: An avenging angel sends a pestilence on Israel because of David's transgressions, and the angel urges David to erect an altar to Yahweh.

2 Chronicles 32.21: An angel strikes down all the battle commanders of the king of Assyria and peace comes to Jerusalem.

Tobit 5.4-28: Tobias encounters the angel Raphael, who comforts his aging father and protects Tobias on his journey

Tobit 6.2-8.9: The angel Raphael assists Tobias in finding a wife.

Tobit 9.1-9: Raphael helps Tobias with the wedding feast.

Tobit 11. 7, 8: Raphael promises Tobias that his blind father will see again.

Tobit 11.14: On having his sight restored, Tobit prays, "Blessed be God! ... Blessed be all his holy angels!"

Tobit 12.6-22: Raphael instructs Tobias and Tobit on spiritual matters and "they were both overwhelmed with awe." Assuring them not to be afraid, he leaves them to return to God's home.

Job 1.6-12: Satan sets out to test Job.

Job 2. 1-10: Satan brings more misfortunes onto Job, who utters no sinful words.

Job 4.18: God finds fault in his own servants "and even with his angels."

Psalm 8.5: "You have made humans a little less than the angels."

Psalm 34.7: The angel of Yahweh keeps safe those who fear Yahweh.

Psalm 35.5, 6: "May the angel of Yahweh chase and hound my enemies," cries the psalmist.

Psalm 78.25: In eating manna from heaven, the Israelites "ate the bread of the angels."

Psalm 78.49: Angels of disaster have carried out God's anger toward the Israelites at times.

Psalm 91.11: God will protect you by putting you under the care of his angels.

Psalm 103.20: "Bless Yahweh, all his angels…"

Psalm 104.4: "You use the winds as messengers and flames of fire as servants.

Psalm 106.37: Israelites under pagan influences sacrificed their children to demons

Psalm 148.2: "Praise Yahweh, heavenly heights, praise him, all his angels, praise him, all his armies!"

Ecclesiastes 5.5: Do not tell your angel that your own words are unintentional.

Isaiah 37.36: An angel of the Lord strikes down thousands of men in the Assyrian camp overnight.

Isaiah 63.9: A psalmist sings of how "it was neither messenger nor angel but God's Presence" that saved the suffering people of Yahweh.

Daniel 3.28: An angel saves three men from the fire of King Nebuchadnezzar.

Daniel 6.22: Daniel attributes his being saved from the lion's jaws to the intervention of an angel.

Hosea 12.4: The prophet recalls Jacob's wrestling with an angel in Genesis 32.24-28.

Zechariah 1.9-2.3: The prophet has visions in which angels play a significant part in passing on messages from Yahweh to the people of Israel.

Zechariah 3.1-6: The angel of Yahweh presides over a court of justice in heaven, and Satan, the accuser, who is man's enemy, stands next to the high priest Joshua.

Zechariah 4.1-6, 10-14: An angel explains a vision and its meanings, including the seven eyes of Yahweh "that cover the whole world" and the two anointed ones who "stand before the Lord of the whole world."

Zechariah 5.5-11: An angel explains a vision concerning wickedness.

Zechariah 6.4-8: An angel explains a vision concerning four great horses going out into the four directions, "the four winds of heaven"—they are to "patrol the whole world."

Zechariah 12.8: In the messianic age the House of David will be restored and "like the angel of Yahweh."

II. CHRISTIAN BIBLE

Matthew 1.20-24: An angel appears to Joseph in a dream and tells him about Mary's conception by the Holy Spirit, counseling him to take Mary as his wife.

Matthew 1.24: Joseph wakes from his dream and does what the angel advised.

Matthew 2.13, 14: An angel appears to Joseph in a dream and warns him to escape from Herod by taking his wife and child into Egypt. Joseph obeys.

Matthew 2.19-2 1: Following Herod's death, an angel appears to Joseph in a dream and tells him to return to Israel, which Joseph does.

Matthew 4.1-11: Jesus is led into the wilderness and tempted by the devil. He resists and we are told, "The devil left him, and angels appeared and looked after him."

Matthew 7.22: Some will say that they cast out demons in Christ's name.

Matthew 8.16, 17: He cast out devils and cured many sick people.

Matthew 8.28-34: Jesus casts out demons from two demoniacs from Gadarenes.

Matthew 9.32-34: Jesus casts a devil out of a man who was mute.

Matthew 10.8: Jesus admonishes his disciples to "cast out devils."

Matthew 11.18: John came and was accused of being "possessed" by the devil.

Matthew 12.22-28: Jesus cures a blind and dumb demoniac, and the Pharisees say that only the prince of devils can cast out devils.

Matthew 13.39-41: In explaining the parable of the good seeds sown in the field, Jesus says that the devil is the enemy who sowed bad seeds and the angels are the reapers. The Son of man at the end of time "will send his angels," who will gather evil and throw it into a blazing furnace.

Matthew 13.49: At the end of time the angels will separate the wicked from the just.

Matthew 15.22-28: A Canaanite woman asks Jesus to heal her daughter who is tormented by a devil and Jesus does so.

Matthew 16.23: "Get behind me, Satan; you are an obstacle in my path," says Jesus to Peter.

Matthew 16.27: "The Son of man is going to come in the glory of his Father with his angels" to reward persons according to their behavior.

Matthew 17.14-20: Jesus cures a boy who is a lunatic and possessed by a devil.

Matthew 18.10: The little ones have "their angels in heaven [who] are continually in the presence of my Father in heaven."

Matthew 22.30: At the resurrection men and women do not marry but are like the angels in heaven."

Matthew 24.31: The Son of man will come on clouds of heaven and "will send his angels with a loud trumpet" to gather chosen ones from the four winds and all directions.

Matthew 24.36: Neither angels nor the Son but only the Father knows the day and hour of the final coming.

Matthew 25.3 1: Angels will escort the Son of man when he comes in his glory.

Matthew 25.41: An eternal fire prepared for the devil and his angels awaits those who refused to feed the hungry or visit the sick and imprisoned.

Matthew 26.53: When arrested in the garden of Gethsemane Jesus says to his disciples that the Father could send him "twelve legions of angels" to defend him if he so wished.

Matthew 28.2-8: An angel of the Lord rolls away the stone to Jesus' tomb and tells Mary of Magdala and Mary of James that Jesus has risen and how they should tell the other disciples.

Mark 1.12, 13: Jesus was tempted by Satan in the wilderness following his baptism, but "the angels looked after him."

Mark 1.32-39: He cast out devils and cured many

Mark 3.15: He appointed disciples "with power to cast out devils."

Mark 3.22-30: Jesus confronts those who accuse him of being Satan who casts out Satan.

Mark 5.1-20: At Gadarenes Jesus cures a man overcome with unclean spirits "and everyone was amazed,"

Mark 6.13: The twelve disciples cast out many devils and cured many sick people.

Mark 7.25-30: Jesus casts the devil out from a pagan woman's daughter.

Mark 8.38: The Son of man will come in glory with his holy angels.

Mark 9.38, 39: A man who was not a disciple was casting out devils in Jesus' name.

Mark 12.25: Those who rise from the dead will not marry but be like the angels.

Mark 13.27: The Son of man will send the angels to gather the chosen from the four winds and the ends of the earth.

Mark 13.32: But the day and hour of that coming even the angels do not know.

Mark 16.9: The risen Christ appears to Mary of Magdala, "from whom he had cast out seven devils."

Mark 16.17: "In my name my followers will cast out devils," says the risen Christ.

Luke 1.11-25: The angel Gabriel appears to Zechariah and informs him that his elderly wife, Elizabeth, will bear a son named John.

Luke 1.26-38: The angel Gabriel tells Mary that she will bear a son named Jesus by the power of the Holy Spirit. Mary consents.

Luke 2.9-15: The angel of the Lord appears to shepherds at night with news of great joy" to be shared by all the people: "Today in the town of David a savior has been born to you; he is Christ the Lord." A great host of angels appears singing, "Glory to God in the highest."

Luke 2.2 1: At his circumcision Jesus is given the name the angel gave him before his birth.

Luke 4.1-13: The devil tempts Jesus in the desert wilderness.

Luke 4.33-36: Jesus orders an unclean spirit to leave a possessed man who is in the synagogue.

Luke 4.40, 41: He laid hands on persons and devils came out of them.

Luke 7.33: John the Baptist is accused of being possessed.

Luke 8.2: Mary of Magdala had seven demons cast out of her.

Luke 8.12: The seed as word of God is taken away by the devil from those on the edge of the path.

Luke 8.26-39: Jesus drives out the demons from the man from Gadarenes.

Luke 9.1: Jesus called the Twelve and gave them power over all devils and to cure the sick.

Luke 9.26: The Son of man will come "in the glory of the Father and the holy angels."

Luke 9.37-45: Jesus drives out the unclean spirit from the boy epileptic demoniac.

Luke 10.17-20: "The seventy-two came back rejoicing, 'Lord,' they said, even the devils submit to us when we use your name.'"

Luke 11.14-22: Jesus confronts those who say that he drives out demons with the help of demons.

Luke 12.8, 9: Those who declare themselves for Christ openly will be openly declared "in the presence of God's angels."

Luke 13.10-17: Jesus heals a crippled woman on the Sabbath, a "daughter of Abraham whom Satan has held bound for eighteen years."

Luke 13.32: Jesus tells the Pharisees to tell Herod that he is casting out devils.

Luke 15.10: "There is rejoicing among the angels of God over one repentant sinner."

Luke 16.22: In the story of Lazarus the poor man dies and is "carried away by the angels to the bosom of Abraham."

Luke 20.36: Those who are resurrected do not marry and "are the same as the angels."

Luke 22:31: "Simon, Simon! Satan, you must know, has got his wish to sift you all like wheat."

Luke 22.43: An angel comes to Jesus in the garden of Gethsemane "to give him strength."

Luke 24.23: Persons on the road to Emmaus discuss how women who visited Jesus' tomb did not find the body but saw "a vision of angels who declared he was alive."

John 1.51: Jesus tells Nathanael that he will see "heaven laid open" and "the angels of God ascending and descending."

John 5.4: An angel is said to enter the pool to stir up the healing waters at the pool of Bethesda.

John 6.70, 71: "One of you is a devil," says Jesus, referring to Judas, who would betray him.

John 8.44: Jesus confronts his enemies and says, "The devil is your father" and "he is a liar, and the father of lies."

John 8.48-54: Jesus is accused of being possessed by a devil.

John 10.20, 21: Jesus is accused of being possessed by a devil and thus of being mad.

John 12.29: When Jesus prays, "Father, glorify your name!" and a voice from heaven says, "I have glorified it," people standing by attribute this to an angel speaking to him.

John 13.2: At the Last Supper "the devil had already put it into the mind of Judas Iscariot" to betray Jesus.

John 20.12, 13: Mary sees two angels at Jesus' empty tomb and one asks her, "Woman, why are you weeping?"

Acts 5.3: Peter asks Ananias, "How can Satan have so possessed you that you should lie to the Holy Spirit?"

Acts 5.19-21: The angel of the Lord frees the apostles from prison and tells them to "tell the people all about the new Life." They do as instructed.

Acts 6.15: Stephen's face before the Sanhedrin appears to be "like the face of an angel"; thus a kind of theophany for transfiguration experience is suggested.

Acts 7.30, 35, 38: Stephen's discourse recalls how Moses was amazed to see "an angel appear to him in the flames of a bush that was on fire." Through Moses, the Jewish people communicated with the angel.

Acts 7.53: In his speech Stephen says to the people that angels brought the law to them.

Acts 8.26: The angel of the Lord tells Philip to set out on a journey and he does.

Acts 10.3-8, 22: A centurion named Cornelius had a vision in which an angel of God told him to go find Simon Peter. He sends his men to do so.

Acts 10.38: Peter preaches and says, "Jesus went about doing good and curing all who had fallen into the power of the devil."

Acts 11.13: Peter recalls the role of the angel in Cornelius's vision to fetch him.

Acts 12.7-15: An angel of the Lord delivers Peter from prison. (See page 182.)

Acts 12.23: An angel of the Lord strikes Herod with a sickness that kills him.

Acts 13.10: Paul confronts the magician Elymas and calls him a "son of the devil" and an enemy of all true religion.

Acts 23.8, 9: At Paul's trial before the Sanhedrin a split arises between the Pharisees, who believe in angels, and the Sadducees, who do not.

Acts 26.18: Paul gives a speech and says that we are to move "from the dominion of Satan to God."

Acts 27.23-26: Paul calms his shipmates who are adrift in the sea with the news that an angel of God assured him that no lives would be lost at sea.

Romans 8.38, 39: Paul is certain that nothing—"neither death nor life, no angel, no prince ... not any power ... can ever come between us and the love of God made visible in Christ Jesus our Lord."

Romans 16.20: "The God of peace will soon crush Satan beneath your feet."

1 Corinthians 4.9: "We have been put on show in front of the whole universe, angels as well as men."

1 Corinthians 5.5: Satan will destroy a person who is living with his father's wife.

1 Corinthians 6.3: We are also to judge angels.

1 Corinthians 7.5: Satan might tempt married couples.

1 Corinthians 10, 20-22: Sacrifices of idols is food offered to demons, who are not God.

1 Corinthians 11. 10: Out of respect for the angels, women are to cover their heads in church assemblies.

1 Corinthians 13.1: "If I have all the eloquence of men or of angels, but speak without love, I am simply a gong booming or a cymbal clashing."

2 Corinthians 2.11: "We will not be outwitted by Satan."

2 Corinthians 11.14, 15: Paul speaks of Satan disguising himself as an angel of light as do certain counterfeit apostles.

2 Corinthians 12.7: Paul's thorn in the flesh is also called an angel of Satan.

Galatians 1.8: Paul tells his readers to ignore preaching that is different from what they have already heard, even if it be from an angel.

Galatians 3.19: "The law was promulgated by angels."

Galatians 4.14: Paul feels he was welcomed "like an angel of God" by the Galatians when he was sick.

Ephesians 4.27: You will "give the devil a foothold" if you let the sun set on your anger.

Ephesians 6.10-13: Our struggle is against "the sovereignties and the Powers. ... the spiritual army of evil in the heavens" and not just against human enemies.

Colossians 2.18: "Do not be taken in by people who like grovelling to angels and worshipping them; people like that are always going on about some vision they have had."

1 Thessalonians 2.18: Paul says Satan prevented his visiting his brothers in Thessalonika.

2 Thessalonians 1. 7: When the Lord Jesus appears from heaven with the angels, those who injure you will be repaid.

2 Thessalonians 2.9-12: Satan will set to work with deceptive signs and portents when the Rebel comes.

1 Timothy 1.20: The writer says he has handed men "over to Satan to teach them not to be blasphemous."

1 Timothy 3.6, 7: The leader of the local church should not be a proud person who "might be condemned as the devil was condemned,"

1 Timothy 3.16: Christ "was made visible in the flesh, attested by the Spirit, seen by angels."

1 Timothy 4.1: Some will listen to deceits and lies that come from the devil.

1 Timothy 5.15: Owing to scandal, some have already left to follow Satan.

1 Timothy 5.21: "Before God and before Jesus Christ and the angels he has chosen" Paul admonishes Christians to behave themselves.

2 Timothy 2.26: The devil catches people and enslaves them, but they can be rescued from this trap.

Hebrews 1.4-14: Christ is far above the angels, and the author invokes Scriptures to demonstrate his point.

Hebrews 2.2: The law was a promise made through angels.

Hebrews 2.5-9: Angels will not rule the world to come. Citing the psalmist, the author says that Jesus is the one who "for a short while was made lower than the angels."

Hebrews 2.14: By his death Christ took away all the devil's power.

Hebrews 2.16: "It was not the angels that he took to himself; he took to himself descent from Abraham."

Hebrews 12.22: In the city of the living God, millions of angels gather for festival.

Hebrews 13.3: In welcoming strangers, "some people have entertained angels without knowing it."

James 2.19: Demons believe and tremble with fear. Belief requires deeds.

James 3.15: A heart of jealousy and ambition is devilish.

James 4.7: "Resist the devil and he will run away from you."

1 Peter 1.12: "Even the angels long to catch a glimpse" of the Good News of Christ.

1 Peter 3.22: Christ has made "the angels and Dominations and Powers his subjects."

1 Peter 5.8: Be vigilant against your enemy the devil.

2 Peter 2.4: "When angels sinned, God did not spare them."

2 Peter 2.11: Some people are so self-willed that they offend angels; yet the angels hold off accusing them before God; the reward for their evil will follow later.

1 John 3.8: The Son of God appeared to undo all that the devil has done.

1 John 3.10: Distinguish children of God from children of the devil.

Jude 6: Certain angels had supreme authority but failed to keep it and were expelled from their sphere of influence.

Jude 9: The archangel Michael argued with the devil.

Revelation 1.1: The source of the Book of Revelation is an angel sent by God to make things known to the author, John.

Revelation 1.20: The seven stars and the seven churches are under the control of angels.

Revelation 2.1-7: "Write to the angel of the church in Ephesus and say…"

Revelation 2.8-11: "Write to the angel of the church in Smyrna and say…"

Revelation 2.12-17: "Write to the angel of the church in Pergamum and say…"

Revelation 2.18-29: "Write to the angel of the church in Thyatira and say…"

Revelation 3.1-4: "Write to the angel of the church in Sardis and say…"

Revelation 3.5: In the presence of the Father and the angels certain people will be acknowledged.

Revelation 3.7: "Write to the angel of the church in Philadelphia and say…"

Revelation 3.9: There are persons who say they are Jews but are not, and these the author calls "the synagogue of Satan."

Revelation 3.14-22: "Write to the angel of the church in Laodicea and say…"

Revelation 5.2: A powerful angel asks whether there is anyone worthy to open the scroll and break its seals.

Revelation 5.11, 12: In a vision tens of thousands of angels were shouting and singing around the heavenly throne.

Revelation 7.1-3: The author sees four angels standing at the four corners of the earth and another angel rising where the sun rises and warning the four angels not to damage the land or sea or trees until a seal is put on the foreheads of the servants of God.

Revelation 7.11, 12: All the angels in a circle around the throne were worshiping God.

Revelation 8.2-10.11: Seven angels in heaven sound their seven trumpets. Each has its own powerful message to tell. An additional angel stands at the altar of incense and prays with all the saints and shakes the earth by the fire from the altar.

Revelation 9.20, 21: Many people refused to give up worshiping devils.

Revelation 11.15: The seventh angel sounds his trumpet and voices in heaven shout: "The kingdom of the world has become the kingdom of our Lord and his Christ, and he will reign forever and ever."

Revelation 12.7-17: In the vision, war breaks out in heaven and Michael and his angels attack the dragon. The devil's days are numbered, but he pursues the woman of the male child and others on earth.

Revelation 14.6-11: Three angels are seen. One calls all peoples to fear God and praise him; another calls out, "Babylon has fallen"; and a third exclaims that those who worship the beast will drink God's fury.

Revelation 14.15-20: Angels reap the harvest of the earth and gather the vintage of the earth into the winepress of God's anger.

Revelation 15.1-8: Seven angels bring seven plagues but also harps and hymns from Moses, along with seven golden bowls that contain the anger of God.

Revelation 16.1-21: The seven angels empty the seven bowls of God's anger over the earth.

Revelation 17.1-18: An angel shows the author how the "famous prostitute," the Roman empire, will be punished for its many sins. "The woman you saw is the great city which has authority over all the rulers on earth."

Revelation 18.1-3: Another angel shouts of the fall of Babylon.

Revelation 18.21-24: Another angel hurls a boulder into the sea and declares that Babylon will be destroyed like that boulder.

Revelation 19.17, 18: An angel standing in the sun calls birds to gather at the great feast.

Revelation 20.1-3: An angel descends from heaven and overpowers the devil and Satan, chaining them up for a thousand years.

Revelation 20.7-10: After a thousand years Satan will be released from prison and will swarm over the country but will be thrown into the lake of fire and sulfur forever.

Revelation 21.9-15: An angel shows the author the holy city of Jerusalem radiant and coming down from God out of heaven. An angel carried a gold measuring rod to measure the city and its gates and wall in the heavenly Jerusalem.

Revelation 22.6-15: An angel tells John of the truthfulness of his writing and warns John to worship God and not him and not to keep prophecies secret. "Happy are those who treasure the prophetic message of this book."

Revelation 22.16: "I, Lord Jesus, have sent my angel to make these revelations to you for the sake of the churches."

NOTES

★ ★ ★

PREFACE

1. "Angels Among Us," Time, December 27, 1993, 56-65.

INTRODUCTION

1. *Summa Theologiae* 1, q. 50, a. 1; q. 63, a. 7.

2. Matthew Fox, *Sheer Joy: Conversations with Thomas Aquinas on Creation Spirituality* (San Francisco: HarperSanFrancisco, 1992), 161.

3. For an account of this hypothesis, see Rupert Sheldrake, *A New Science of Life: The Hypothesis of Formative Causation* (3rd ed; London: Icon Books, 2009) and *The Presence of the Past: Morphic Resonance and the Habits of Nature* (2nd ed: Rochester, Vermont: Park Street Press, 2011).

4. See, for example, Timothy Ferris, *The Mind's Sky: Human Intelligence in a Cosmic Context* (New York: Bantam, 1992).

5. Ferris, *Mind's Sky*, 31.

6. London: Chapman and Hall, 1911.

7. Matthew Fox, *The Coming of the Cosmic Christ* (San Francisco: HarperSan Francisco, 1988).

CHAPTER 1: DIONYSIUS THE AREOPAGITE

1. Dionysius the Areopagite, *The Celestial Hierarchies, in Mystical Theology and the Celestial Hierarchies*, trans. the editors of The Shrine of Wisdom (Surrey, England: The Shrine of Wisdom, 1965), ch. XIV, 60. All citations from Dionysius are from this text unless otherwise indicated.
2. Ch. 111, 29, 30.
3. Ch. IV, 32-34.
4. Ch. VII, 38-39.
5. Ch. XIII, 57.
6. Ch. VIII, 43-44.
7. Ch. XI, 46-49.
8. Ch. XIII, 56-57.
9. Ch. XIV, 62-63.
10. Ch. XIV, 67.
11. Ch. XII, 53-54.
12. Dionysius the Areopagite, *The Divine Names*, trans. the editors of The Shrine of Wisdom (Surrey, England: The Shrine of Wisdom, 1957), ch. VIII, 69-70,nn.1,5.
13. *Celestial Hierarchies*, ch. XV, 65.
14. Ch. XV, 66-67.

CHAPTER 2: ST. THOMAS AQUINAS

Citations from the *Summa Theologiae* (ST), unless otherwise noted, are from the translation in *St Thomas Aquinas: Summa Theologiae* Vol. 9 (New York: Blackfriars, in conjunction with McGraw-Hill Book Company, 1964).
1. ST 1, q. 63, a. 7.
2. ST 1, q. 61, a. 3.

3. ST 1, q. 62, a. 9, ad. 2.

4. ST 1, q. 58, a. 3.

5. Cited in Matthew Fox, *Sheer Joy: Conversations with Thomas Aquinas on Creation Spirituality* (San Francisco: HarperSanFrancisco, 1992), 185.

6. ST 1, q. 58, a. 3.

7. ST 1, q. 58, a. 4.

8. Cited in Fox, *Sheer Joy*, 201.

9. Cited in Fox, *Sheer Joy*, 2 1.

10. ST 1, q. 50, a. 1.

11. ST 1, q. 50, a. 2.

12. ST 1, q. 5 1, a. 1.

13. ST 1, q. 50, a. 4.

14. ST 1, q. 51, a. 2.

15. ST 11, q. 172; cited in Fox, *Sheer Joy*, 470-471.

16. ST, a. 2.

17. ST, ad. 1.

18. ST, ad. 3.

19. Cited in Fox, *Sheer Joy*, 466.

20. Cited in Fox, *Sheer Joy*, 216-217.

21. Cited in Fox, *Sheer Joy*, 16 1.

22. *Quaestiones Quodlibetales (Quod.)*. 1, 4.

23. ST 1, q. 52, a. 2.

24. ST 1, q. 52, a. 2.

25. ST 1, q. 60, a. 2.

26. ST 1, q. 60, a. 5

27. ST 1, q. 52, a. 3

28. ST 1, q. 53, a. 1

29. ST 1, q. 53, a. 2

30. ST 1, q. 53, a. 2

31. ST 1, q. 53, a. 3

32. *Quod.* XI, 4.

33. ST 1, q. 54, a. 4

34. ST 1, q. 57, a. 2

35. ST 1, q. 57, a. 4 36. ST 1, q. 57, a. 3

37. ST 1, q. 61, a. 3

38. ST 1, q. 62, a. 4

39. ST 1, q. 62, a. 1

40. ST 1, q. 62, a. 2

41. ST 1, q. 62, a. 3

42. Cited in Fox, *Sheer Joy*, 119,

43. Cited in Fox, *Sheer Joy*, 515.

44. ST 1, q. 62, a. 3

45. ST 1, q. 62, a. 5

46. ST 1, q. 63, a. 2

47, ST 1, q. 63, a. 3

48. ST 1, q. 63, a. 6

49. ST 1, q. 63, a. 7

50. ST 1, q. 63, a. 9

51. ST 1, q. 63, a. 7

52. ST 1, q. 63, a. 8

53. ST 1, q. 64, a. 4

CHAPTER 3: HILDEGARD OF BINGEN

1. Hildegard of Bingen, *Liber Vitae Meritorum* (Pitra, 1882), 24.

2. Hildegard of Bingen, *Wisse die Wege Scivias* 111, 4.

3. Hildegard of Bingen, J. P Migne, ed. *Patrologia Latina* (PL) (Paris: Migne,1844-91), 197, 229C.

4. PL 197, 262D. 5. PL 197, 889A.

6. PL 197, 917B.

7. *Liber Vitae Meritorum*, 444.

8. PL 197, 917B.

9. PL 197, 746C.

10. *Liber Vitae Meritorum*, 157,

11. PL 19 7, 442A.

12. *Liber Vitae Meritorum*, 352.

13, *Liber Vitae Meritorum*, 217.

14. *Liber Vitae Meritorum*, 75.

15. PL 197, 960D-961A,

16. PL 197, 812B.

17. PL 197, 812B.

18. PL 197, 812B.

19. PL 197, 170A.

20, *Liber Vitae Meritorum*, 36 1.

21, *Scivias* 111, 1.

22. PL 197, 747C.

23. *Scivias* 11, 2.

24. *Scivias* 111, 1.

25. PL 197, 272D.

26. PL 197, 945C.

27. PL 197, 865D.

28. PL 197, 1061C.

29. PL 197, 236C.

30. PL 197, 1041C.

31. PL 197, 1045A.

32. Hildegard of Bingen, *Causae et Curae* (Leipzig: P Kaiser, 1903), 26, 53.

33. *Scivias* 1, 1.

34. PL 197, 898B.

35, PL 197, 898D.

36. PL 197, 1043A.

37. PL 197, 1043C.

38. *Scivias* 11, I.

39. See Matthew Fox, *Breakthrough: Meister Eckhart's Creation Spirituality in New Translation* (New York: Doubleday, 1980), 77.

40. PL 197, 946B.

41. *Scivias* 1, 4.

42. *Scivias* 11, 6.

43. *Liber Vitae Meritorum*, 320.

Index

Printed in the USA
CPSIA information can be obtained
at www.ICGtesting.com
JSHW082202140824
68134JS00014B/373

9 781939 681287